Profit-Driven Business Strategy

Using Cost and Profit Numbers to Dominate your Market

Randy MacLean

Profit-Driven Business Strategy
Using Cost and Profit Numbers to Dominate your Market

First Edition

ISBN: 978-1530087457

www.randymaclean.com

Table of Contents

Introduction

This book is the culmination of much of the advisory work I've been doing for our clients over the past decade.

In working with some of the smartest and most capable executives in business, and with the help of the deep experience of partner, friend and mentor, Bruce Merrifield, I've had the great fortune to accumulate a broad understanding of strategies and tactics that work, and also those that fail.

A year before beginning to commit the contents of this book to paper, I began to think about how all of the things you've learned about taking a numbers-driven approach to making profit fit into the broader context of market position and market share.

You've seen companies led by executives that created an inflection point and put their companies into stellar and sustained profit growth. What part of their thinking and activities resulted in the eye-popping 174% average profit gain they delivered to their stakeholders?

You've also seen executives captured by their own history and unable to effect the constant change needed for the financial health of all organizations. They're actively planning for a return of the "good ol' days" while their business is being eaten away by younger (or at least younger-thinking) competitors. What are these companies doing that's playing into the hands of the competition?

Those of you who know me, or have heard me speak, know how important whale curves are to a coherent understanding of business profit generation, and these are the very genesis of this book. For the better part of a decade, I've been dedicated to helping our clients understand and utilize whale curves to maximize their profit generation.

Accepting that every market has finite limits, it follows that market players are continually engaged in a zero-sum game. That is, my competitor's gain can only come at my expense. So I stepped back to a market level, and asked two questions.

What are the worst things a competitor could do to my whale curve?

What are the best things I can do to improve the profit realization of my own whale curve?

To answer these questions, I had to go back to everything I've learned about profit analysis and profit-generation practices. I also rediscovered some of the deep wisdom in Michael E. Porter's timeless and ground-breaking 1980 book, Competitive Strategy (ISBN: 0-02-925360-8), which has given me an edge in business for over three decades. Most importantly, I could rely on the collective wisdom and the real-world results of executives that have delivered profit and sales growth gains that far exceed market norms.

In the answers, I not only found the common threads that drive profit gains in today's environment, I also discovered the vital importance of executing the steps in the right order, for without this discipline great harm can be done to a company's profit line.

The result is this book, where I can share the six-step strategy that can give any company a distinct and substantial edge, putting profit and market gains on a steep and sustainable upward trajectory. The company's competitors will become largely helpless to counter the strategy, finding themselves in a fight for survival.

For "numbers guys" like me, a warning. Given some of the conventional wisdom you've all worked within, some of the strategy elements may seem counter-intuitive. This is largely or wholly due to one factor -- you can't do the math in your head. The assumptions underlying the short-cuts needed for mental arithmetic simply prevent accurate conclusions. In this book, I'll walk through the actual mathematics that drive profit and profit gains. Those that can make the transition will get an intuitive and instinctive understanding that can be applied broadly to drive incremental profit gains.

Note: Throughout the book, I'll be making liberal references to our system, WayPoint Analytics. I make no apologies for this, as I make my living helping executives use the information from WayPoint to deliver profit rates 2x–4x industry standards, and the reports from the system most directly illustrate the principles and methods that support the strategy the book is about.
I've included a short section at the end for those wanting to know more about WayPoint Analytics, and I do hope it'll become your tool of choice to measure, monitor and manage profit.

Why a Profit Strategy?

Why is it so important to implement a new strategy? You've probably been using the same strategy for some time and it may even be institutionalized within your business. This strategy is probably working pretty well for you—since you've managed to stay in business all these years—and, if you're like many business leaders, you may wonder why you can't just stick with your existing strategy forever.

The simple answer is because things change. While your strategy may have helped to make your company the best in your area or worked extremely well with certain customers, you live in an ever-changing world. Customers change, competitors change, products change, everything changes, and if you aren't changing with it, you may find your company left behind.

As the world becomes more sophisticated, more information is becoming available and people are gaining new insights by paying closer attention to this data. They can use this data to determine what does or doesn't work. It's giving companies like yours a deeper understanding of why certain activities have a positive or negative effect.

Because the world is changing at an increasingly rapid pace, business leaders need to start thinking about how they plan for the future whether it's strategy for the next five years, two years, or this year. Let's start by defining strategy.

Jonathan Byrnes, a MIT lecturer and incredible strategic thinker who consults with some of the largest companies on the planet, gave me the following words of wisdom many years ago: "If you don't say 'No' to anything, you don't have a strategy." What this means is that strategy is defined not only by what you do but, more importantly, what you *don't* do.

Many companies believe they have a strategy in place when they really just have a nebulous idea that involves pursuing good opportunities. However, you can't excel at pursuing the good deals if you're wasting time chasing the bad ones.

Jonathan's words crystallize the importance of understanding and communicating your company's direction. Your employees need to understand what your company does and doesn't do so they can devote their time, energy, and resources into the things that work.

This brings us to another important lesson. If you're going to thrive in a competitive environment—whether you're a CEO trying to take the business in a new direction, a company trying to sell more into the marketplace, or just looking to get a raise (or promotion)—then you need to be better than the other guys.

This doesn't mean that you have to be perfect in everything you do. You just need to spend more of your time working on things that matter and bring you closer to your goals than everybody else. If you fritter away less of your time on things that distract or prevent you from getting where you want to be, you'll wind up spending a larger proportion of time on the things which will help you get there. This greatly increases the likelihood that you'll achieve your goals before anybody else.

Prioritizing the things that matter over everything else is the cornerstone of any good strategy. You need to understand exactly what you're trying to achieve. You need to recognize the things that help you get there and the things that distract you from your goal. And, in order to properly execute this strategy, you need to make sure that everybody in your organization understands these things and are working on them as well.

In the past, strategies were built on somewhat limited information. Companies either lacked data or the ability to process the wealth of data available. You've turned a corner thanks to advancements in technology which, combined with new information and ways of thinking, have provided astounding insights into the mechanisms that help companies make and lose money.

You may be interested to learn that this trend is common in just about every kind of business and in every industry. Many of the widely-held beliefs that most of us were taught when coming up the ranks are based on bad or incomplete information. Whether you're a salesperson or a CEO, there's a very good chance that you're laboring under some misconceptions.

The most important epiphany is that all businesses are the sum total of their money-making activities and money-losing activities. While this idea is obvious on a surface level, obtaining a deeper understanding on a more visceral level can help to guide anybody towards working on the most important things. To foster this understanding, I want to make a point about making and losing money.

In distribution, the economics of any sale, division, or territory really boils down to two things: the amount of Gross Profit dollars that are being generated and the cost-to-serve dollars spent in delivering those products or services.

When the Gross Profit dollars being generated are greater than the cost-to-serve expenses, the sale is profitable and the gains contribute to the bottom line.

However, if you have sales where the cost-to-serve is greater than the Gross Profit, then you're going to be generating loss on that sale or in that territory with that customer. What that means is you wind up with a sale somewhere in the company, even if it's just a single invoice, where you lost money because you haven't brought in enough gross profit to cover the costs associated with delivering the product into the customer's hands. These money-losing sales detract from the profit that you've already made on sales which had a better profit ratio.

How much of the average distributor's business is money-losing? The sheer size of the answer is shocking. Had you asked me to guess 10 years ago, I might have said that 10 to 15% of a business's transactions lose money. However, the reality is far, far larger. Once we ran the numbers, we found that, in wholesale distribution in North America (across all sectors), over 62.5% of all invoices lost money!

I want you to take a second to process that.

Within your own company right now, there's a very good likelihood that 60% of all the invoices being written are basically siphoning money that you've already made somewhere else from the bottom line. This proportion is large enough to induce a panic attack!

However, there's some good news. The silver lining is that anything done so poorly, where only 40% of it is effective, can very easily be changed in a radical way if somebody just begins to understand and manage the process.

There are companies that make two to four times the profit of other businesses selling the same product to the same customers in the same market in the same way. These companies have doubled, tripled, or even quadrupled their profitability by reversing the ratio of profitable business compared to unprofitable business.

Instead of 60%+ of their invoices losing money, these companies get it down to 40% or less. This helps to make the companies world leaders by allowing them to outperform their associations, markets, and industries by a wide margin.

Anybody can do this if they just get in touch with how the numbers work and follow the right strategy. This strategy involves using what you know about how money is made and lost in your business to focus in on the things that make money while doing less of the things that lose money.

It doesn't matter how large or small your company is, you can take over your entire marketplace if you just get disciplined, work hard, and work smart using these kinds of numbers.

And I hope you do.

Managing Change

Implicit in developing and implementing a new strategy is the idea the company and its people will be doing something they're not doing already. In other words, *some things will change.*

Resistance from Process & Attitude

Working against this, every team has a certain level (usually, a high level) of institutional inertia embodied in its processes and the thinking of its people. On the plus side, this is what keeps very necessary activities running in a reliable and predictable way. On the minus side, it also works to prevent necessary adjustments and improvements.

The inertia is particularly strong in organizations that feel they are (or have been) successful. The people will reflexively attribute past success to their thinking and processes, and expect any change will be detrimental.

Change can't be driven through mandate—it can only come when the company starts by changing both the thinking of its people and the procedures that drive their activities.

What Got You Here Won't Get You There

In a rapidly changing market environment, this can be deadly, because it will prevent otherwise capable organizations from keeping the leadership position that past innovations (read that as "change") gave them in the first place.

If you're in your fourth decade in business, you can remember when it took a decade or more for a major change (like "computerizing") to occur. Or later, eMail which took about three years. Now, things like eCommerce, Amazon, smart phones, tablets, and especially profit analytics are changing the game nearly overnight.

Because of the increasing pace and importance of what's changing outside your doors, change management is a critical core competency for every executive.

You Can't Get Different Results by Doing the Same Thing

The successful implementation of a new strategy will require consideration of, and modifications to, how the company operates.

Everyone needs to understand and embrace the idea that getting and holding a leadership position absolutely *requires* the company and its processes to change with (or ahead of) the market.

Every person resisting this fundamental is actively preventing the company's future success.

In previous phases of my career, I led some pretty successful sales teams. If I was asked to lead another of these, I could call on my experience and past successes to mount another terrific program—perfect for the 1990's. And I'd probably get creamed.

Be sure *you're* not the one leading the change-prevention department by holding your team to the now-ineffective practices of yesteryear.

Training the Sales Force

The sales force operates at the "customer-contact surface" of the business. It, and the concierge service team I'll be suggesting later, conduct the bulk of the customer interaction and are on the front lines of nearly everything in the strategy.

For a successful implementation, your company will need to bring the sales team on board, give them the training and tools to execute, and weed out those who will try to impede the company's progress.

This is vital, as there's almost no conceivable path to success without the active and enthusiastic participation of sales.

Profit-Driven Sales Incentives

The most important element of the strategy is identifying and acting on the major accounts which contribute the most profit or drain profits away. It's almost assured that you are currently paying handsomely for money-losing accounts which are actively bad for your bottom line, *and the reps will not want this to change.*

To eliminate this dynamic, and for the purpose of rewarding the reps that engage in profit-generating activities, I highly recommend that you also consider switching to profit-driven sales commissions.

There's a complete roadmap for this kind of program in my 2015 book, Profit Driven Sales Commissions, available at Amazon. (More information at my website: www.randymaclean.com.)

Gain-Sharing

In the end-state of this strategy, you'll have built a new culture that understands and reveres profit. A valuable tool in getting there is across-the-board rewards for the entire team.

I suggest you reserve a share of your newly-found profit for rewarding the team for making the change, and reinforcing the benefit and value of maintaining it.

One company implemented this particularly well, paying a $6,000 gain-sharing bonus to every team member from warehouse to CEO. This wasn't actually very expensive—it was funded out of a profit increase of over $75,000 per employee!

Get Help

Driving real and sustained change really requires special skills, and I highly recommend using an outside expert to help. This, because nearly every failed strategy has the inability to effect change at the core of the failure.

Profit Principles & Metrics

Before you can have an effective profit-driven strategy, it's necessary to have a modern understanding of how profit is actually made (it's not what you've been taught), and the best-available methods and metrics for quantifying and managing it.

For the past decade, I've had access to tens of millions of invoices and corresponding financial statements for over $60B of distribution company business. I've also had the great fortune to have had the brilliant insights and collective wisdom of experts like Bruce Merrifield, Brent Grover, Jonathan Byrnes, Al Bates, Jeanne Hurlbert and many others.

In running thousands of analyses, correlating and applying them to both successful and failed programs and initiatives, our research has identified critical metrics and some rather surprising insights into how companies make (and lose) money.

This has led to a very different understanding of how to manage and control the profit generation of a business. Companies who've gained these insights and adopted the methods they suggest have produced record profits and growth, becoming market leaders overnight.

In this chapter, I'll share the more important of these ideas.

Understanding the "Bottom Line"

There's a fundamental and widely-held misunderstanding that absolutely hampers more executives in their quest for profits.

I think it's rooted in an exercise nearly every young manager has completed early in their career—answering the question, "What's a good sale?"

Knowing, perhaps, the company needs, say, a gross margin of 22% to cover its costs, the answer would be something like, "Any sale with margin above 22%."

This is problematic on its face because it's certainly not the case the cost-to-serve (CTS) on *every* order is 22%, so orders with CTS above 22% are patently *not* "good sales". In reality, gross margin is typically in a fairly narrow range (10%-40%), while corresponding CTS covers practically the whole spectrum (near-zero—300% or more).

More importantly, since it seems possible to ensure that all (or most) sales have a margin of at least 22% and will generate a profit, it seems logical to conclude the company profit will be made up of all the small profits from the individual sales. It's also apparent that since there are few sales with margins below the magic 22%, there's little need to think about those.

This logic leads to the idea that increasing profit is best accomplished by increasing the number of sales.

Sound familiar?

The reality is much, much different!

In distribution, more than 62.5% of invoices are money losers. That is, the CTS on the invoice is greater than the GP, producing a loss.

This means in most companies five invoices of every eight contribute a loss to the bottom line!

This is the source of the first important insight in managing profit: the bottom line is the sum of all the profitable sales and all the unprofitable sales.

Introducing the Whale Curve

By far, the most effective way of visualizing how profit is made is the "whale curve".

A whale curve is simply the chart of an accumulated profit report, but it has the power to instantly communicate a new and accurate idea of how profits are made.

figure 4.01—typical whale curve

The curve climbs on the left, showing profits accumulating from profitable sales, flattens along the top and it accounts for sales that neither make or lose money, and then descends on the right as it reflects increasingly large losses from money-losing sales. It ends when every sale is accounted for and the tip of tail reflects the company's bottom-line number.

There are several important and surprising insights provided by the chart:

- ✓ the company makes a *whole lot more than its actual bottom line* on the best of its sales (roughly four times its bottom line in this example, which is typical)
- ✓ a fair proportion of the company's business produces a loss (roughly 20% of the business, and likely 60+% of the invoices)
- ✓ the bulk of what the company makes on the best is consumed by the losses on the worst

The curve here is absolutely typical of nearly every company. Working from these insights, every management team could make significant changes to their company's profit picture.

> Takeaway: your company very likely has a very large and untapped profit potential right in its existing operations.

The Role of Gross Profit

In the WayPoint environment, Gross Profit ($GP) is a measure of dollars left from revenue after the Cost of Goods is deducted.

This is the money that provides (or actually is) the operating budget for: the company; the branch; the territory; the account; or the individual sale.

Gross Profit provides cash flow to cover the cost of operations, and needs to be preserved and grown where *profitable* conditions exist. (More about this in the next section on Cost-to-Serve.)

The Role of Cost-to-Serve

Cost-to-Serve (CTS) is made up of the operating costs associated with: the company; the branch; the territory; the account; and the individual sale. CTS excludes one very important category of costs—sales compensation. (See the section on NBC to find out why.)

Every sale (and every aggregation of sales) has its own CTS. A sale is only *profitable* when the GP exceeds CTS, and in the majority of sales, this is not the case, the sale actually hurts cash flow and profits.

The Role of Gross Margin

Gross Profit Margin (or Gross Margin, or GM%) is the percentage of Revenue remaining after product costs are covered.

In the absence of a robust set of management metrics, GM% has taken on mythic proportions in the thinking, planning and decision-making of most managers and executives.

The Gross Margin metric is so widely misunderstood and misused, it commonly damages and confounds the profit initiatives intended by companies and their executives.

The measure has been largely taken to be an indicator of profit, but it's simply useless for that purpose. This is because profit is actually created by the spread between GM% and CTS%. (i.e. 25% GM on 18% CTS = +7%; or 25% GM on 31% CTS = –6%)

Without accounting for the actual CTS%, there's simply no mathematical way to know whether any given GM% produces a profit or not. Statistically, most invoices have a CTS%

greater than the GM%, so it can't be left to chance—it needs to be managed.

The proper purpose for GM% is to evaluate or calculate price for a product or account in a way that affects the $GP expected or needed for profitability. *It has no other management purpose.*

Takeaway: Gross Margin % is a very poor way to run anything other than to set price levels and drive $GP for cash flow.

The Role of Transaction Counts

Cost-to-Serve can also be called "operating expense". It's really the cost of manpower and infrastructure needed to provide products and services to customers.

The cost and scale of this is completely controlled by the number of *transactions* it supports. In the WayPoint universe, transactions are: orders; picks; invoices and shipments.

Every expansion in infrastructure and manpower is driven by increases in transactions, and CTS is directly driven by transaction counts.

This insight provides a marvelous insight into how companies can safely and effectively control costs—*control the transaction counts that drive costs.*

You can quickly do a gut check on this.

Does it seem logical that an account that buys the same quantity of the same products, but combines orders into fewer shipments, would have lower costs and be more profitable? Of course.

Transaction counts drive CTS, and are the nearly-unmanaged metric that provide the greatest opportunity for every company to affect and manage profit at every level of business.

> Takeaway: Controlling costs is effectively and safely accomplished by controlling transaction counts. Reducing the need for a given level of infrastructure and manpower allows growth without new investment, or clears the way to make cuts without affecting customers.

Introducing NBC

In our early research into profit-drivers and sales pay, you encountered several near-insurmountable problems with the most common metrics in use.

Solving that collection of problems suggested the invention of a powerful new metric that has become one of the most effective management tools in use today—Net Before Compensation (NBC).

The solution was deceptively simple, create a new metric that includes all operating expenses, but excludes sales compensation. It can best be seen in a simplified P & L format:

	Revenue
–	<u>CoGS (Cost of Goods Sold)</u>
=	GP (Gross Profit)
–	<u>CTS (Cost-To-Serve or Operating Expenses)</u>
=	**NBC (Net Before [Sales] Compensation)**
–	<u>Sales Compensation</u>
=	NBT (Net Before Taxes)

figure 4.02—enhanced P&L with NBC

The new NBC metric solved a number of important analytical and management issues:

- ✓ due to the broad variation in sales pay versus performance, inclusion of sales compensation confounded useful and comparable profit analysis
- ✓ calculation and comprehension of profit-based sales pay was difficult or impossible when the pay itself affected profit
- ✓ there was no good management metric to replace the broad misuse of GM%—one that would account for the critical cost side of profit measurement

NBC% is the modern replacement for GM%, giving managers at all levels an advanced metric that covers both production and costs ($GP & $CTS or GM% & CTS%).

Sales, in particular, benefits from using NBC, because it covers the three controllable elements of the sales, where GM% covers only one. This measure accurately integrates the benefits of the three controllable elements:

- ✓ $NBC is increased if $Revenue is increased
- ✓ $NBC is increased if GM% is increased
- ✓ $NBC is increased if $CTS is reduced

Further, $NBC indicates the profit remaining after the product is paid for, and all operating costs and overhead are covered, leaving an amount to pay the sales rep and the company. If NBC is negative, the GM% and CTS% are out of balance, as operating costs exceeded $GP.

> Takeaway: NBC is the very best management metric for running a territory, a branch or a whole business. Adopt and use NBC to communicate expectations and results. Where sensible, answer questions with something like, "What's the NBC impact of that?" If people need NBC numbers to communicate with you, they'll begin to think in terms of NBC.

Account Profit Dynamics

Since all businesses operate by providing goods or services to customers, it's useful (actually, crucial) to recognize that all customer relationships are not equal—some are much, much more profitable (for both sides) than others. Conversely some are mutually and deeply unprofitable (usually for both sides as well).

Unprofitable relationships are mostly caused by the inability to assess dysfunction in the profit drivers of the relationship, meaning they can quickly and easily be made mutually beneficial (and profitable) with little effort.

Some relationships are inherently unprofitable due to a business model that unduly favors the customer, and these can be difficult or impossible to change into a "win-win".

High-Potential Accounts

Amongst your customer base are a small subset that provide enough business to individually impact the profit performance and cash flow of the company. You call them High-Potential Accounts (HPAs).

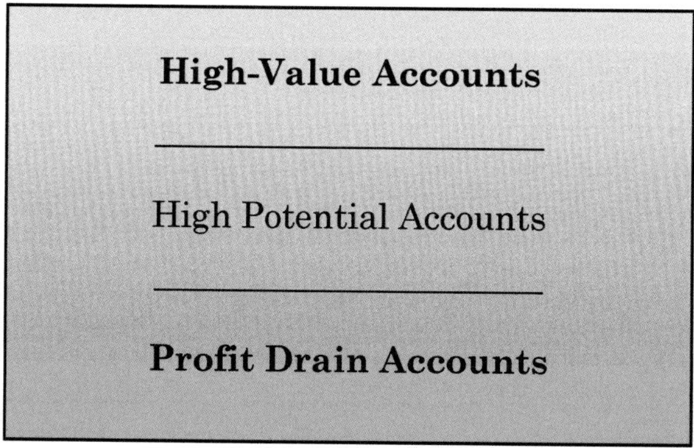

figure 4.03—High-Potential Accounts include High-Value Accounts & Profit-Drain Accounts

HPAs are those that drive above-average Gross Profit dollars ($GP), and they're the account group that absolutely controls a company's operating budget, cash flow, and profits or losses. The accounts in this group are not only those that drive the profits getting to bottom line, they're also the accounts which consume it, depriving the company of profits it's already earned.

For this reason, you further identify two important subsets of the HPA accounts: High-Value Accounts (HVAs) and Profit-Drain Accounts (PDAs).

High-Value Accounts

High-Value Accounts (HVAs) are the cream of the crop—they provide the bulk of the operating profit that drives cash flow. This subset of the High-Potential Account group plays a vital role in profit production.

HVAs are the subset of HPAs that provide nearly all the profits made in the business. These accounts are the most efficient high-GP-volume accounts. They simply consume much less of your company's infrastructure and resources (per unit of revenue) than everyone else.

Every viable company has at least a few of these accounts, and the top companies *are* the top companies because they have an outsized roster of these accounts.

Mathematically, these accounts will (like all HPAs) have above average $GP, but they stand out from others in the HPA group by having below-average Exp%. These are high-volume accounts with high-efficiency, reflected in the low expense rate. They're the exclusive inhabitants of the left side of your whale curve (Zone 1).

Simply stated, they produce more Gross Profit per expense dollar than regular accounts.

These accounts are, by far, the most valuable assets of any company, and the fastest path to profit growth and cash flow improvement is in expanding this group.

Takeaway: HVAs are vital (and in their own category) because they generate an inordinate amount of actual, usable profit. They're the account class vital to the financial health and future of every business.

Profit-Drain Accounts (PDAs)

Profit-Drain Accounts are the evil twins of HVAs, and are severely detrimental to a company's ability to produce profit and cash flow. This subset of the High-Potential Account group limits every company's profit production.

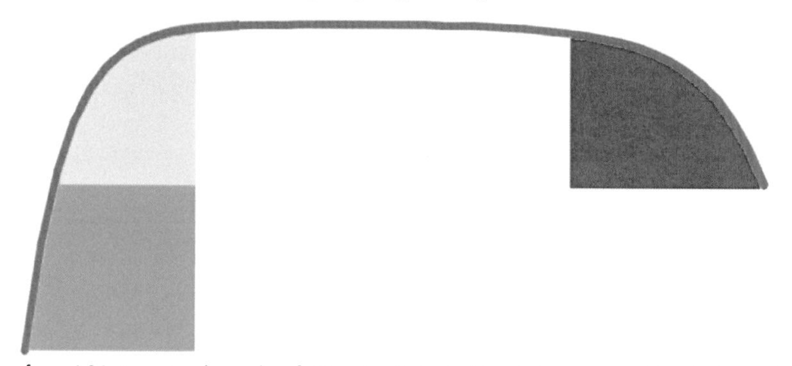

figure 4.04—increasing the number of HVAs raises the back of the whale curve and adds to the bottom line

Almost every company has a collection of PDAs, and this group simultaneously represents both a great profit opportunity, and a drag on a company's ability to produce profit at all.

The PDAs are found on the right side of the curve, creating losses that burn profits already made. The HVAs and the rest of the HPAs inhabit the left side of the curve where profits are made.

Takeaway: Your PDAs are the greatest threat to your company's profit generation, and must be considered in any profit strategy.

High-Potential Products / Services

There's a product-related analog to HPAs / HVAs / PDAs.

With the advent of advance costing and profit analytical systems like WayPoint Analytics, companies are getting access to new product-related metrics that show profit rates inherent in not the product itself, but *in how it tends to be sold.*

For instance, if a particular item is almost always sold with two or three other products that share the same invoice and the same delivery, it will be more profitable than when it's sold individually.

If there's a particular customer group or demographic that tend to buy more of their product less frequently and on larger orders, the products they buy will be measurably more profitable in these circumstances.

There will also exist customer / product combinations that are the opposite of these two scenarios.

These inferred relationships are demonstrated in the most advanced profit analytics, and this can be exploited to increase company profits.

Because if this, you can identify High-Potential Products (HPPs), High-Value Products (HVPs), and Profit-Drain Products (PDPs).

Takeaway: When considering your product line strategy, evaluating the profit impact of HPPs is a powerful guide to future gains.

Working Without Advanced Analytics

In an environment where you don't yet have an advanced costing and profit system like WayPoint Analytics to directly report the HPAs / HVAs / PDAs, you can still use what you know to work the strategy.

The first stage in the process involves identifying the high-volume or high-velocity accounts. These are accounts which generate large amounts of gross profit dollars which, depending on their associated cost-to-serve, turns into either profits or losses. Consequently, you can achieve tremendous results by more efficiently managing these accounts.

The way you segment or identify these accounts will vary. Depending on the size of your business, you might look at your top 50 or top 100 accounts. You could also choose a threshold based on gross volume, such as looking at accounts which generate $100,000 a year, or $500,000 a year. The method you choose will naturally depend on the scale of your business and the kinds of accounts you service, but you should be looking at accounts which generate large amounts of profit.

It's important to remember that you can't make or lose a significant amount money on a small account. On the other hand, the accounts at the top of the gross profit production list, the ones generating the most gross profit dollars, are going to either massively contribute to your profitability or massively detract from it. If the cost-to-serve is way out of proportion with those accounts, they can easily drain a lot of profit from your bottom line.

The accounts with above average profit rates, meaning the NBC rate is above the company average rate, are ones that you want to preserve.

The accounts which have above average gross profit production but produce losses, especially large losses, need attention right away. You want to work on these accounts first in order to close off some of the profit drain. These are all service-drain accounts, meaning they use more service and your logistics than their business pays for. The money lost on these accounts eats away at the profits made on your best accounts and keeps that money from reaching the bottom line.

Business Models

In looking at the way a company does business with each kind of account, there's a particular way of collecting together what the company does and doesn't do. This is what you think of as a "business model" or "service model".

For instance, a common business model could be described like this: Sales reps call on accounts, obtaining orders that are fulfilled through the warehouse, delivered (at no charge) on company vehicles, and the monies are collected thirty days later.

There's an infrastructure component (and related cost) inherent in each part of the model described above.

Consideration of, and proper planning of, business or service models is an important profit-management activity covered later in this book.

Strategy Roadmap

The strategy I'm suggesting in this book is designed to give any company adopting it a significant and permanent advantage in their market.

It will keep them focused on the things that drive profit, and help avoid the things that destroy it.

In a nutshell, the mission is to get in control of the company's whale curve, and change its shape into one with a much larger profit-generating Zone 1 on the left, and a much smaller money-losing Zone 3 on the right.

Competitive Strategy

Because every company operates in a market environment with finite limits, share and profit gains will come at the expense of your competitors, which tends to amplify and accelerate the process. This means the competition won't be happy.

When executed properly, the improvements are permanent and sustainable. As long as your company doesn't let the new disciplines slip, the competition cannot reverse the process to recover what they'll be losing.

The high-level view can be summarized in just six steps, but it's essential they be executed in order. This, because it's quick and easy to shed Gross Profit ($GP) in the middle steps, but risky (and probably destructive) to do so before building new $GP from activities in the early stages.

You Can Have It All

Most of us have heard something along the lines of, "price, service, profits: pick two". With a modern and sophisticated view of cost and profit analytics, this is no longer the case.

Because every business is largely supported by super-profitable segments, there's easily enough cash flow to support all three—provided the company loses the profit-draining segments that normally consume the extraordinary profits generated on the best business.

This is heart of the strategy, and the purpose of this book.

Strategy Steps

It's vital to recognize that certain steps increase $GP while others will reduce it. Overall, the intent is to *replace* dysfunctional and profit-draining $GP with profitable $GP.

For this reason, the steps in the strategy emphasize building replacement $GP before giving up (or driving off) the business that's bad for profits.

Warning—be sure you don't get the steps out of order, or your implementation *will hurt your cash flow*.

The strategy steps are:

1) create concierge-level customer service
2) protect the cash & the profit core
3) add new cash flow and profit
4) ditch the profit drains

5) use pricing to lock high-value business
6) actively manage account trading
7) refine or develop business models

Step 1: Concierge Customer Service

The early phases of the strategy contemplate both protecting the best existing business, and acquiring more. Both of these are best done by providing a differentiating business reason for accounts to stay, or to join your customer roster.

I believe Concierge Customer Service is one of the business reasons which will distinguish you for top accounts.

I'm using the "Concierge" qualifier to differentiate it from what most companies think of as "customer service"—an order-entry group.

Although nearly every executive believes his company provides good "customer service", this is no truer than most parents thinking their children are "above average intelligence". Clearly, half must be below-average for the average to be an average.

If you're not putting a fair amount of continual effort into measuring and improving your customer's experience with you, which half of companies is yours likely a member of?

Creating a tangibly-better customer experience is perhaps one of the more fun and interesting things executives can work on. It's not only well-suited to the "servant's heart" every successful entrepreneur must have, it's also the source of great pride in imagining how the best customers can be surprised and delighted in being served by the company.

Meanwhile, there's an important strategic intent in concierge customer service—it has a number of business purposes:

- ✓ to deliver a "customer experience" beyond expectations, and beyond competitors' capabilities, creating a reason for the customer to stay with your company
- ✓ have a mechanism to identify and quickly resolve problems so they don't become an irritant in the relationship
- ✓ generate additional communications with the customer to spot and exploit opportunities
- ✓ solicit testimonial feedback for marketing
- ✓ create additional relationship value salespeople can leverage to win new accounts

What I Mean by "Concierge"

When using the term "concierge", I'm thinking of the experience I've had when speaking at an event at one of the country's actual five-star hotels.

The car at the airport is a 600-series Mercedes; there's no line at the special check-in and the clerk offers a hot towel before beginning the check in; everyone calls me "Mr. MacLean"; no one will allow me to carry my bags; a car to shopping is complimentary… and a hamburger is $50.

I use the term "customer experience" because it clearly articulates the desired result: a good feeling about your company, driven by the feeling of being treated like an important customer. The customer is left with the impression the company values them, cares about their company, and thinks about what it's like to be them.

When properly executed, the customer feels some loyalty and attachment to the company, and has a preference or bias toward doing business with the company. It's the emotional glue that holds customers when the imperfect parts of an imperfect world occur.

Takeaway: For your most valuable customers, create a team to deliver a "customer experience" that creates a bias or preference for doing business with your company. This will become one of the business reasons your team will use to attract top accounts.

For Only Select Accounts

This business model is based on providing an exceptional level of service, for a select group of customers that appreciate, *and will pay*, to get it.

Let me put this another way—this kind of service is provided to a select group of customers that provide the extraordinary levels of cash flow to pay for it *and* return a profit to the company.

No company can create and maintain this kind of service for every account, excepting those with a service model built exclusively for high-volume, high-profit business. (Like many five-star hotels.)

Building a Bias

The first purpose of the Concierge Service step is to build a new capability to distinguish your company from its competition.

The strategic intent is to have a valuable and durable business reason to choose your company over others, and to make this a differentiating tool in the hands of the sales force.

You'll be creating a concierge service team intended to deliver a new, and much better "customer experience".

I like the term "customer experience" because it clearly articulates what the desired result is—a good feeling about the company, driven by what it feels like to be an important customer. The sense the company values me, cares about me, and is thinking about what it's like to be me.

Early Warning

Implicit in Concierge Customer Service is a high level of communication between your company and the customer.

This will provide an unusual early warning capability that can detect and correct issues in your performance before they have a chance to harm the relationship.

In fact, quickly-corrected issues can have an unintended benefit—they provide a noticeable opportunity for the customer to see how your company responds to the challenges that become irritants in their relationships with your competitors.

Trading & Gravity

Nearly every company operates in an environment where there's a continual and on-going inherent trading process as customers move between suppliers.

The gravitational pull of a well-executed and maintained concierge program more quickly attracts new accounts and makes them slower to leave if they leave at all.

Marketing Advantage

Companies that take the most sophisticated approach to customer service extend their customer communications in a way that actually *generates* new testimonials.

This extraordinary step has given many of our clients a significant advantage by providing power and credibility to their marketing programs.

Sales Advantage

In the hands of a capable sales organization, the advantages of a noticeably-superior customer service capability can be parlayed into rapid sales and profit growth.

They're no longer trying to persuade customers through personal rapport-building, but instead have tangible business reasons and credible marketing backup to convince target accounts to change sides.

How it's Done

If you want to differentiate your company from the pack, you need world-class service. Thus the first stage in implementing any good strategy involves creating a concierge service team designed to deliver a new, superior "customer experience."

Developing and maintaining a team that delivers a tangibly-better customer experience is one of the most interesting and fulfilling tasks that an executive can undertake. It strikes a chord within the "servant's heart" that beats within every successful entrepreneur's chest. Many executives take immense pride in imagining how the best customers will be surprised and delighted by a company's service.

While a customer's gratitude is enough for some distributors, it's worth noting that concierge customer service carries a number of strategical, practical benefits. By delivering a "customer experience" beyond their expectations—and anything the competition could offer—you're creating a powerful incentive for making your customers want to stay. It also provides you a mechanism for identifying and immediately resolving problems before they become a serious issue. The additional communications with your customer will help you spot and exploit new opportunities.

The feedback the system generates can also be used for testimonials. These provide a powerful social proof for your marketing efforts. Finally, the process creates additional relationship value that salespeople can leverage to win new accounts.

Simply put, Concierge Customer Service (or CCS for short) is an incredible tool for retaining your best accounts. However, some of the benefits will "trickle down" throughout your company, even changing its culture, because the system will provide feedback from everybody and can help you streamline your service to make it more efficient.

Additionally, in the same sense that your service can be used to attract new customers, CCS can be used to upgrade some of your current customers. If a customer sees the program and likes how it works, he may want access to the same, higher-level service. This can be used as leverage to change the nature of your relationship with the customer, convincing him to give you either additional business or to conduct business in a way that makes his business is more profitable.

One thing to keep in mind is that CCS may represent a radical change in a company's thinking. It's part of a broader approach to take companies from a product-centric point of view to a more customer-centric one. While it's a significant change, it's also a critical one. This system can prove absolutely essential when it comes to retaining customers. If you're using it, your competitors will have a very hard time getting your accounts. Conversely, if your accounts are taken by a competitor who has their own CCS system in place, you'll have a tremendously difficult time trying to recover those accounts (or get new ones) from that competitor.

The Chief Customer Officer

Many top companies have started to take the customer-centric approach seriously. In 2003, fewer than 20 companies world-wide had a Chief Customer Officer. As of 2015, more than a fifth of all Fortune 100 companies as well as more than a tenth of Fortune 500 companies have appointed a Chief Customer Officer.

What does a Chief Customer Officer do? He or she ensures the company has a deep understanding of their customers or clients; builds lasting relationships with those customers; and creates and operates continuous-improvement programs to keep Concierge Customer Service evolving into the future.

How to Get Help

It's outside the intended scope of this book, and beyond my expertise to provide the detail and best practices for setting up your company's concierge customer service program.

However, I can provide you with access to some introductory materials from Hurlbert Consulting, who've guided many of our clients to very successful implementations of the precise program envisioned here.

www.ConciergeCustomerService.com

Summary

Create a concierge customer service capability:

- ✓ select and train at least two people
- ✓ dedicated space, phone, email, authority
- ✓ customer advocates
- ✓ "own" customer's issues, and report status to customer
- ✓ plan for customer-caused issues
- ✓ continuous survey
- ✓ consider having a Chief Customer Officer
- ✓ get expert help

Step 2: Protecting your GP

Gross profit production is the initial activity in which your company engages with the customer. It provides the operating budget for your company; or your branch; or your territory.

It funds everything you do.

Some $GP is associated with a low CTS, and leaves a profit after expenses are covered. In most companies, the majority of $GP is associated with CTS greater the $GP itself, driving losses that consume profits already made on better business.

The currently-profitable portion of your business must be considered and protected as you roll out initiatives to support your strategy.

Business where the CTS cannot be brought into line to produce profits is the very definition of business best in the hands of your competition. At some point you want to give up this business, but *not* before replacing it with profitable $GP.

Why This Matters

Some time ago, a company launched an initiative that changed policies and pricing for small accounts. The letter announcing the policy changes was sent to the entire customer base.

This caused wide and very negative blowback, as nearly every customer came to the conclusion the new policies would apply to them (they wouldn't have), and competitors began using the new policy letter to get accounts riled up so they'd switch away.

The customer service (order entry) staff that had the most contact with the customer base were blindsided, and naturally sympathized with the upset customers inadvertently reinforcing the controversy.

The policy change itself was well-considered, but poorly executed.

In a better execution, the company would have taken additional steps:

- ✓ target the policy letter only to the small subset of accounts which would be affected
- ✓ provide a mechanism in the policy that would have given the accounts a way to avoid the impact of the policy change by modifying how they worked with the company
- ✓ simultaneously send an explanatory letter to all other customers letting them know they'd not be affected by the change
- ✓ brief the customer service and account rep teams, providing scripts they could follow to work with customers that misunderstood or disputed the changes, putting the change in a positive light

The main point here is to consider the impact of each initiative of the strategy in light of customer impact and perception. Ensure that as you proceed, nothing adversely affects cash flow.

Your Whale Curve

Switching to the high-level view of what you'll be working to accomplish, it's useful to think of your company's whale curve.

If it's typical, you're making very good money on about 10%–15% of your total business, and losing about 75% of those profits on about the worst 25%.

This means your Peak Internal Profit (PIP) is roughly 4–5 times your bottom line. These are profits you already have in hand—they're just being whittled away by the 60%+ of your transactions that lose money.

figure 7.01—typical whale curve

Your strategic objective is to begin to actively manage the profit-generation mechanics of your company to change the shape of the curve.

I'll show how to identify the dynamics that drive the profit generation on the left, the hollow activity along the top of the curve, and the dysfunctional, money-losing business on the right.

Certain portions of the money-losing business can be changed into money-makers, transferring then off the right side and increasing the upslope on the left, raising the height of the curve while reducing the amount of the downslope. This will create more cash flow and a bigger bottom line.

Adding new money-makers to the left, also raises the height of the curve and contributes to cash flow and profit.

Finally, eliminating some of the unfixable money-losers on the right cuts cash flow, but cuts expenses at a greater rate.

figure 7.02—post-strategy whale curve with a profit rate three times the initial rate

The end-state curve has more high-profit business and less money-losing business, and results in profit rates roughly three times the initial rate—on similar or slightly increased revenue.

Takeaway: Understanding what your whale curve gives you a powerful insight to help appreciate, protect and build on the extraordinary profits your company already creates.

Launch your Concierge Service Program

The curve is driven by HVAs in the lower section of the left side, HPAs in the upper part of the left and extending slightly in to the top, and PDAs on the right side.

Knowing this, the first place to extend your new concierge customer service capability is to the HVAs.

Develop materials for the program, train the sales force on it, and have them call on the accounts to introduce both the program and the service team.

Solicit and inventory outstanding issues with the HVAs and HPAs, and put these into the hands of the service team for resolution.

Then, where possible increase the sales tempo with these accounts, or have the service team initiate frequent contact to "check in", handle issues and report back.

High-Potential Accounts

	Customer	Revenue	GP			Exp		NBC		Invoices	Type
		$	$	%	/inv	$	%	$	%	Total	
1	I Party Retail Store	1,040,103	122,682	11.8%	449	46,402	4.5%	76,280	7.3%	273	HVA
2	12th Street Ht Associatates LP	863,280	119,337	13.8%	512	48,828	5.7%	70,509	8.2%	233	HVA
3	Uniland Partnership of Del LP	412,012	61,835	15.0%	824	15,627	3.8%	46,208	11.2%	75	HVA
4	Kilian Mfg Co	180,164	50,752	28.2%	558	13,221	7.3%	37,531	20.8%	91	HVA
5	Premier Seating Company	207,863	59,261	28.5%	507	27,739	13.3%	31,522	15.2%	117	HVA
6	Disc Graphics Inc	254,517	56,961	22.4%	459	26,804	10.5%	30,157	11.8%	124	HVA
7	Columbia Communications Corp	226,799	33,655	14.8%	3,739	4,353	1.9%	29,301	12.9%	9	HVA
8	Dynamics Research Corporation	321,999	48,499	15.1%	379	19,860	6.2%	28,639	8.9%	128	HVA
9	Kelley Steel Erectors Inc	231,400	54,974	23.8%	341	30,680	13.3%	24,294	10.5%	161	HVA
10	Medical Life Insurance Co	160,121	57,275	35.8%	444	33,151	20.7%	24,123	15.1%	129	HPA
11	Equitrans L P	173,538	36,860	21.2%	498	13,098	7.5%	23,762	13.7%	74	HVA
12	David Penske Chevrolet Inc	244,558	59,598	24.4%	355	48,807	20.0%	10,791	4.4%	168	HPA

figure 7.03—High-Potential Account report in WayPoint

Summary

At the end of this step, you'll be taking several steps to lock in the core of your gross profit production to protect your cash flow and prepare for the coming steps of the strategy.

- ✓ inventory and resolve outstanding HPA issues
- ✓ increase contact and responsiveness to strategically-important HVA and HPA accounts
- ✓ roll out concierge customer service to HVA and HPA accounts

Step 3: Build GP

The next important step is to build money-making Gross Profit (as opposed to the money-losing Gross Profit already present due to the PDAs).

This is largely because you'll later want to lose the unreformable part of the account base that is unlikely to ever be profitable. Avoiding the cash flow impact of the later step absolutely requires that you create replacement cash flow first.

Increasing Account Penetration

Going back to your entire HPA list, you'll task the sales force with increasing penetration of the HVA / HPA / PDA list. Specifically, I mean selling more into these accounts.

Despite the inevitable claims of the reps, few of your accounts are likely to be buying everything they could from your line, and these accounts will be the easiest places to acquire new GP.

Since all of these accounts represent significant GP velocity, nearly all can post GP increases without any corresponding CTS increase. This means a portion of these accounts will move up the value list just through this action. (HPAs will become HVAs, and PDAs can become HPAs.)

See the sales force has a closer look at all the HPAs and make sure there's no opportunity to sell into these top accounts which's being missed. There's every opportunity to increase gross profit production using the same cost structure, as long as no incremental business brings a larger incremental cost.

Since no account is ever buying everything they can from you, a little legwork, or sometimes just asking, can deliver nice increments in sales and profits.

> Takeaway: Increasing $GP through account penetration is the fast first step in building "replacement" $GP.

Targeting New Accounts

A very powerful next step is to increase the number and quality of money-making HPAs.

Examining an NBC profit ranking report, or an HPA Account report shows the best current profit contributors, and it's a good bet these customers' direct competitors have a high likelihood of being the same.

Sales can use Concierge Service and, potentially, pricing to target the most likely accounts, and can offer aggressive (but profitable) price points, provided certain efficiency standards are met. This is a lot less complex than it sounds...

The call might include something along these lines...

> *"We provide our line to a lot of companies like yours, and we think we have the best service available. In fact, we're so sure of it we'd like to offer special pricing as long as you're respectful of the amount of our resources you use. Your pricing is about 2.5% lower than normal 'best price' as long as each order is at least $2,500 and you require no more than one shipment per week. In*

addition, we'll pay your shipping on the first two shipments each month."

This ties aggressive pricing into a model that controls CTS and looks like other HVAs. (You'll do your own math to find out what the numbers need to be for your environment. The WayPoint High-Potential Account report is a great starting point.)

Poaching HVAs

I'd also like to point out an apparent paradox that opens a whole new avenue for sales focus. Looking at an NBC Profit Ranking report (figure 8.01), you'll notice the most profitable accounts are not necessarily the ones with the largest revenue. If you look at the top ten accounts here, there's a range all the way from under $22,000 up to over $250,000 in the top ten accounts by NBC in this one territory.

Customer Ranking by Net-Before-Comp (NBC)

	Customer	Revenue		GP			Exp			NBC		Invoices	
		$	/ inv	$	/ inv	%	$	/ inv	%	$	accum	Total	-NBC
1	Medical Life Insurance Co	160,121	1,241	57,275	444	35.8%	33,151	257	20.7%	24,123	24,123	129	65%
2	David Penske Chevrolet Inc	244,558	1,456	59,598	355	24.4%	48,807	291	20.0%	10,791	34,915	168	60%
3	Metropolitan Bank And Trust Co	107,935	1,861	29,280	505	27.1%	20,674	356	19.2%	8,606	43,521	58	26%
4	Telstar International Inc	54,713	1,272	17,336	403	31.7%	12,221	284	22.3%	5,115	48,636	43	35%
5	Millennium Bostonian Hotel	261,580	2,357	43,161	389	16.5%	38,305	345	14.6%	4,856	53,492	111	58%
6	Riggs Distler & Company Inc	25,668	546	16,607	353	64.7%	11,922	254	46.4%	4,685	58,177	47	60%
7	Richardson Myers & Donofrio	43,143	2,054	12,807	610	29.7%	8,126	387	18.8%	4,680	62,858	21	43%
8	Koda Enterprises Group Inc	69,520	2,575	18,600	689	26.8%	14,796	548	21.3%	3,804	66,662	27	33%
9	T & J Development Co	37,778	548	18,196	264	48.2%	14,419	209	38.2%	3,777	70,439	69	58%
10	B A A Pittsburgh Inc	22,738	1,137	5,992	300	26.4%	2,326	116	10.2%	3,666	74,105	20	35%
11	Harrisburg Dairies Inc	23,859	1,988	7,016	585	29.4%	4,003	334	16.8%	3,013	77,119	12	42%
12	Palomar Medical Technologies,...	146,451	2,989	26,347	538	18.0%	23,721	484	16.2%	2,626	79,745	49	69%
13	Womens Marketing Inc	3,250	650	3,026	605	93.1%	532	106	16.4%	2,493	82,238	5	0%
14	Enco Manufacturing Company	13,902	869	6,069	379	43.7%	3,624	226	26.1%	2,445	84,683	16	56%
15	L E K Consulting LLC	5,735	1,434	2,711	678	47.3%	661	165	11.5%	2,049	86,733	4	25%
16	Cfp Holdings, Inc	31,485	2,862	6,715	610	21.3%	4,770	434	15.2%	1,945	88,678	11	45%
17	Moore's Falls Corp	2,848	712	2,501	625	87.8%	639	160	22.4%	1,862	90,540	4	50%
18	George Campbell Painting	33,748	3,375	3,897	390	11.5%	2,325	233	6.9%	1,572	92,112	10	50%
19	Rochester Instrument Systems	5,516	5,516	1,602	1,602	29.0%	433	433	7.8%	1,170	93,281	1	0%
20	Lmac LLC	21,560	392	11,994	218	55.6%	10,890	198	50.5%	1,104	94,385	55	73%
21	Fortran Printing Inc	6,135	1,022	2,352	392	38.3%	1,634	272	26.6%	718	95,103	6	33%

figure 8.01—NBC profit ranking report showing the most profitable customers

The first takeaway is smaller accounts which are run efficiently can be big profit generators, and are usually lightly defended in the competition's hands.

The salesman on the other side is a lot more worried about a large account that buys hundreds of thousands of dollars of product, than the smaller account that takes a fraction of that. He doesn't have a way of knowing the smaller account is just as valuable or, in some cases, more valuable so is not likely actively defending it.

Takeaway: Having the sales team engaged in accumulating new High-Value Accounts (HVAs), or creating them from the existing HPA group, is likely the most productive objective of any company.

High-Potential Accounts

	Customer	Revenue	GP			Exp		NBC		Invoices	Type
		$	$	%	/inv	$	%	$	%	Total	
1	I Party Retail Store	1,040,103	122,682	11.8%	449	46,402	4.5%	76,280	7.3%	273	HVA
2	12th Street Ht Associatates LP	863,280	119,337	13.8%	512	48,828	5.7%	70,509	8.2%	233	HVA
3	Uniland Partnership of Del LP	412,012	61,835	15.0%	824	15,627	3.8%	46,208	11.2%	75	HVA
4	Kilian Mfg Co	180,164	50,752	28.2%	558	13,221	7.3%	37,531	20.8%	91	HVA
5	Premier Seating Company	207,863	59,261	28.5%	507	27,739	13.3%	31,522	15.2%	117	HVA
6	Disc Graphics Inc	254,517	56,961	22.4%	459	26,804	10.5%	30,157	11.8%	124	HVA
7	Columbia Communications Corp	226,799	33,655	14.8%	3,739	4,353	1.9%	29,301	12.9%	9	HVA
8	Dynamics Research Corporation	321,999	48,499	15.1%	379	19,860	6.2%	28,639	8.9%	128	HVA
9	Kelley Steel Erectors Inc	231,400	54,974	23.8%	341	30,680	13.3%	24,294	10.5%	161	HVA
10	Medical Life Insurance Co	160,121	57,275	35.8%	444	33,151	20.7%	24,123	15.1%	129	HPA
11	Equitrans L P	173,538	36,860	21.2%	498	13,098	7.5%	23,762	13.7%	74	HVA
12	David Penske Chevrolet Inc	244,558	59,598	24.4%	355	48,807	20.0%	10,791	4.4%	168	HPA

figure 8.02—High-Potential Account report in WayPoint

The question is: how do you know what accounts the opposing rep has on his profitability list? That's easy. One of the tricks that sales can use is to look at the accounts which are the most profitable on their profit ranking list, then target the direct competition of those accounts. Those are most likely to be accounts which are just as profitable.

If your sweet spot is, say, an air conditioning contractor who has between 10 and 20 trucks on the road, his direct competition is going to be other air conditioning contractors who have 10 and 20 trucks on the road. They're likely going to be run in the same way; they're going to buy the same products in similar volumes; they might even have the buyer that this guy used to have; and they may have a lot of processes in place that make them similar.

So the first thing I would do is look at the top ten or fifteen most-profitable accounts in any territory, identify other companies that look just like them, and then go after those accounts. It's much, much better than just throwing darts at the Yellow Pages or getting the next guy down the street. You have a very good chance of finding another high-potential account if you target accounts which look like your existing high-potential accounts.

Preventing PDAs

In your quest for new HVAs, you should have a mechanism to check incoming target accounts, spotting those which are actually PDAs because they bring a CTS greater than their GP.

Movement of PDAs should be one-way only—to the competition. If you're getting accumulating PDAs, it's possible your competition is working this same strategy against you.

It's also vital that your company has a systemized way to identify and address situations where existing HVAs and HPAs become PDAs. Warning bells should sound, and sales management and the sales team should respond to the scene of the loss, ready to correct the problem.

Money-Losing Invoices

So the second thing I wanted to point out here is there's an absolute correlation between Profit-Drain Accounts and Money-Losing Invoice percentage. (The right-most columns in the report in figure 8.01.)

This provides an important indicator of actions every sales rep can take to improve territory profit. The NBC Ranking report shows, for each account, the number of invoices and what percentage of them lose money. So the best account on the sample report had 129 invoices and 65% of them lost money.

So in terms of changing the profit being generated on these accounts, you can go in and start looking at why are two-thirds of the invoices losing money? What is it about these invoices? What is on these invoices? And is there a way you can work with the customer and make them even more profitable? This is one of the best techniques to get more territory profit and to improve its whale curve.

The largest accounts in each territory present the best and most-leveraged opportunity to get gains, either through selling more or by reducing costs by reducing orders, picks and shipments. Because of the size of the larger accounts, small increments can scale into significant profit gains.

Start with the most-friendly large accounts—the ones you have the best relationship with. Take a look at the bottom of the invoice list for those that lost money to determine what's driving the losses. Is the customer sending a lot of panic orders for small items? Is there a low-value product that's being ordered frequently?

See if you can work with the account to combine orders, find alternate delivery methods or some innovation in the logistics chain that can reduce or eliminate money-losing invoices.

Accomplishing this will free up some of your infrastructure so it can be employed to serve incoming new customers, eliminating the requirement for infrastructure expansion.

Summary

The company needs to build $GP:

- ✓ increase sales to existing high-velocity accounts
- ✓ target likely HVA and HPA candidates
- ✓ increase GP / reduce CTS in existing accounts to make them HVAs
- ✓ utilize the negative invoice metric to improve both account and territory profitability

Step 4: Lose Bad Business

There's a certain portion of every company's customer roster that is simply unprofitable by any measure.

These accounts are most frequently large companies with many locations, and with a business model that requires you to provide additional specialized services or facilities. Due to their size, they also expect below-average price.

These customers are the natural inhabitants of the right side of your whale curve, and can be found at the bottom of every profit ranking report. They're your PDAs.

Your Plan for Fixing PDAs

Your initial goal is to do quick turnarounds on these accounts. Often, you'll see results fairly quickly. In our experience, about three or four of those accounts can be turned around within about 90 days with some discussion and negotiation.

However, these talks need to be handled by somebody near the top of the company. A salesperson would have difficulty in making these reforms because it requires going up against somebody that doesn't have the same vested interest in the profitability of the relationship as a senior executive or owner. Because the decision-makers usually aren't receptive to sales reps discussing these matters, the approach calls for what Bruce Merrifield refers to as a "honcho-to-honcho" call.

For each account in the PDA category, it would be appropriate to develop a specific plan for that account. You want to identify the specific reasons for the account performing so poorly. While the overall problem is always an over-consumption of resources for the amount of gross profit contributed, the specifics will often vary.

You'll find certain classes of accounts in this category. The most common is a "large" company or large account which consists of a number of small operating branches. These branches may even closely resemble your marginal accounts but, because they all have the same name, it hides these branches are effectively very small, money-losing accounts.

Are PDAs Important?

The most common reasons executives give for keeping PDAs are:

1) need the GP from these account to fund operations
2) need the volume to drive rebates
3) need the prestige of having the account

I'll address each of these in turn.

Gross Profit from PDAs

If you've been executing the strategy, you'll have added healthier, more-profitable $GP from elsewhere, so you can now afford to give up these accounts to increase the bottom line without hurting cash flow.

If you can't reform them and you don't give them up, PDAs will be a perpetual drain on your bottom line, and you have little chance of reaching industry-leading profit rates. The ongoing drain will also be a perpetual drag on cash flow.

The cash flow component matters for another important reason. Every company should be free of bank debt, especially an operating line balance. Properly used, an operating line provides a buffer to protect against short-term unforeseen expenses, or to support the pursuit of short-term opportunities.

Too many companies effectively fund long-term financing requirements with a perpetual operating line balance that may have existed for years, decades, or even generations. It may have been the practice of the company so long that it seems "normal", but it a very risky and profit-draining practice.

If this describes your company, the increased profits from this strategy can help it get out of the line, and put the practice into the past where it belongs.

Rebates on PDA Business

I have a very dim view of rebates.

Their very purpose is to distort the market by getting your company to do things it would *never* do if the rebates weren't there. Things like: loading up on inventory; selling product other than what's best for your customer; keeping competitive products from gaining a foothold; etc.

Some companies operate in low-data environments where margin-management is rampant, and rebates allow product costs to be artificially high, hiding profits in the eventual rebates. These companies use rebates as profit insurance.

Companies with better profit information can evaluate their HPAs / HVAs / PDAs, and make money with or without rebates. (They gladly accept the rebate money as a profit enhancement, but it has little or no impact on their decision-making or operations.)

If you manage your HVAs and PDAs effectively, rebates can be a profit enhancement, rather than the profit itself.

Prestige

I've seen many cases where executives value the marquee of PDAs above the profit-consuming impact of these accounts.

In these cases, I'm always at a loss to understand how the holding on to a significantly money-losing account is consistent with the mandate to guide the company to superior performance.

However, continuing to accurately and consistently measure profit impact of these accounts eventually leads to effort to correct the loss or, sometimes, to giving up the account.

Important?

In my view, what's important is fixing, or losing, PDAs.

Takeaway: There's no good rationalization for a PDA—they're simply an unwelcome drain on cash flow and profits.

Some Scenarios from History

There are a number of cases that provide useful illustrations of how others have evaluated and acted on PDAs.

Multi-Location Customer (No Distribution Infrastructure)

An example of this phenomenon might be a national chain which has many locations and the current service model—which was mutually developed—most likely involves shipping small quantities of product to a lot of different locations fairly frequently. Effectively these kinds of customers aren't really large national accounts, but instead a collection of marginal accounts all under one umbrella.

These accounts are marginal in the sense they consume more resources than you could possibly make on the gross profit dollars made from them. They also expect the best price because they think of themselves as being very large because, as an aggregate, they represent a fair amount of business. You and your salespeople may have been thinking this as well.

However, these are the kinds of small accounts which you would never take on unless you had a logistical solution in place that specifically addressed their issues. The most common solution for issues involving large chains is to borrow part of their logistic system.

One example of a large chain issue involved a paper distributor who had considered selling to banks. The president of the company was looking for opportunities and came to the conclusion that banks use more paper than anybody else in the market. However, the challenge with banks was they typically had a lot of locations yet lacked their own logistical distribution mechanism.

While banks could offer a large volume in aggregate, they also carried a much larger cost-to-serve in order to serve the accounts' many locations. The paper distributor ultimately decided to forego selling to banks because they couldn't find a profitable way to work with them.

Bear in mind, this is an extreme example where there was no solution for that kind of customer. They simply could not make the relationship work. This is one perfectly-acceptable, numbers-driven conclusion not in the inventory of some companies.

Multi-Location Customer (With Distribution Infrastructure)

However, this same paper company was able to forge a successful working relationship with some national retailers of office supplies. These retailers also had many locations with separately managed inventories but, unlike the banks, they also had their own logistical system which the paper distributor could borrow. They had their own mechanism to distribute products from their central locations or their distribution centers out to their branches.

The various branches of these national retailers didn't bring in much volume on an individual basis but, as an aggregate, they were quite profitable. More importantly, tapping into the retailers' distribution network drastically reduced the paper distributor's cost-to-serve.

The distributor made incredible inroads into that entire industry by building custom ordering solutions that were convenient, easy, and accurate for the local managers who used them. The electronic ordering process also meant managers wouldn't have to deal with sales reps or a complicated order entry. Likewise, the shipments were bundled in such a way as to make it easy for the customers' distribution centers to move the already-bundled product to their branches using their own trucks and infrastructure.

This paper distribution company had a single truck with a whole bunch of pallets, skids, boxes, or bundles that would bring everything to the customer's distribution center in a single delivery. The customer would then divvy up those orders and combine them with other products headed for their branches and would handle the "last mile" of the deliveries in a much more cost-effective way. It was a logistically efficient solution for both the distributor and the customer. It also served to create an entry barrier for competitors because the distributor had a custom order entry system in place, custom preparation in the pick-pack-and-ship operation, and a place in the customer's logistical system for transport. This was something that no competitor could hope to easily duplicate.

That company held onto the business of large retailers for decades thanks to this kind of system because nobody else could get into the accounts. They had taken some high-velocity gross margin accounts and some money-draining accounts and analyzed the issues with that account. Being willing to innovate, they got "outside the box" and invented a system that solved the problem and gave them a very competitive position.

This is the kind of opportunity that you want to find within your own business.

Customer Segmentation

It's worth noting there's a great deal of work being done in the marketplace on customer segmentation. You can use government SIC or NAICS codes to segment customers by industry and so on.

We have people in the contractor supply business who talk about residential contractors, commercial contractors, retailers, and other customers. Taking a look at different kinds of customers usually helps you understand different kinds of logistical systems you may be using with those customers. It's more closely correlated to cost-to-serve, which is important when it comes to understanding whether customers are likely to be profitable.

On that facet of business, I can say the cost-to-serve rate (i.e. the cost-to-serve dollars or the operating expense dollars—operating expenses being defined as all of the expenses to pay for all of your facilities and operations except for customer-facing salespeople—the rate of that number as a percentage of revenue) is the best determinant of whether a company is likely to be profitable or unprofitable.

When you combine this with segmentation information, you can identify industry trends. For instance, let's look at the tire business. Back in the day, gas stations used to double as auto repair places. They sold gas, but they could also change your oil and had a couple of bays where they could repair your car if it broke down.

These auto service stations would usually buy some tires. If a motorist rolled in the morning and needed a pair of tires, the station would call the tire wholesaler who would deliver the tires within an hour or two.

It was a very expensive way to do business even back when tires cost a lot more or customers paid more than you do now. Nowadays that model is less operational and, as a result, we see fewer of those small service stations because it's very difficult for them to stay in business with today's economy. When you look at the tire wholesale business, you'll see remnants of that old business which has very high costs and are still under margin pressure to reduce prices. It's incredibly hard for either the service station or the tire wholesaler to make money.

When you start to look at whole categories and apply line item profit analytics to customers like these, you would realize this is a segment that either needs a different kind of service model or just isn't viable.

Another tire industry category worth examining is big box stores where a national chain has a lot of locations. If you can't borrow their logistics, it's almost impossible to give them the aggressive pricing they demand in a cost envelope that you can afford. As a result, they might not work out well.

On the other hand, there may be government locations, commercial enterprises, tire specialists, or tire stores that buy tires in large volume and take them in larger quantities on single shipments. Because they're buying in bulk and require fewer shipments, the logistical cost is spread across more product and the cost-to-serve on that class of companies is lower.

Understanding the cost-to-serve rate (or operating expense rate) is a great determinant factor in identifying segments of the business that are likely (or unlikely) to make money. I recommend using this metric to sort the wheat from the chaff when you're trying to assess customers.

Profit Techniques

In this chapter, I've discussed major PDAs and some of the factors that cause these accounts to generate money-losing business. I want to encourage you to start looking for those factors in your PDAs. The idea is to either find a logistical cost-to-serve envelope that allows you to make money on those accounts, change policies to add more gross profit into the accounts, convince them to change their behavior so they'll prefer more financially viable logistical systems or, as a last resort, quietly guide them into the hands of a competitor.

The first objective always is to turn the money-losing account, especially one with significant volume, into a money-making account. The best way to do that is by reducing the cost-to-serve.

The second option is to use add-ons, such as delivery charges and small order fees, to encourage them to change their behavior so they will consume fewer resources, making them more profitable.

The third opportunity involves changing the service model for those accounts so you do business with them in a different way. In the case of accounts having large volumes and very small orders, you could offer them free delivery on just the first shipment of each day.

You could also approach them and explain something along the lines of, "We're going to start charging a $5 invoicing fee to cover our processing costs, so it could get pretty expensive to have us create so much paper on so many smaller orders. Creating invoices costs money, and we're willing to share the cost if you really require them. We have a $10 cost creating and handling each invoice—we'll carry half of it and we want you to carry half of it. And, if you eventually reduce the number of invoices you need, you're going to reduce your cost." Hopefully this will help to modify their behavior or, at the very least, offset some of your costs.

Competitive Effect of Losing PDAs

Ideally, the best of these have already become HVAs (or, at least, not PDAs) through your previous efforts. If they're unwilling to be part of a win-win relationship with you, they need to go.

By far, the best place for an unreformable PDA is in the hands of the competition. It frees your company to focus more on the accounts which pay the bills, while paralyzing your competition as they provide service they can't afford to a customer which will not pay for them.

Adding your roster of PDAs to those already in the hands of your competitor accelerates the drain on his profits and cash flow, and will quickly run out his financing sources. If he doesn't figure it out and stem the bleeding, his future is bleak.

Add his limiting beliefs (the account is large and valuable; all GP is good; get all the business you can; etc.), he'll fight tooth-and-nail to hang on to the money-losing account that's killing his profits and cash flow.

If you've also poached some of his HVAs, he'll have reduced profits to begin with, and this will really compound his problems.

This should give you some peace surrounding the concept of ceding PDAs to the competition.

If you have large volume accounts which simply cannot be made profitable, then it's best to give them up. They can go paralyze a competitor and drain their profits. This allows you to re-deploy those resources on the new incoming accounts which were discussed in the earlier chapters so you don't have to increase head count to accommodate the new business coming in. The employees who were working on the money draining accounts can instead pick up the new workload.

Step 5: Reprice HVAs & Target Accounts

This chapter covers some of the most exciting results to come out of the strategy, including the ability to truly offer it all!

It's something most companies have long wanted to achieve but found the prospect mathematically impossible because they didn't have the right information or the proper, cohesive strategy.

Many distributors are familiar with some variation of the old adage, "Service, Price, Profits. Choose two." This idea represents a practical limitation that made sense to me decades ago, but I've since learned better. You really CAN offer it all. It's mathematically and logistically possible to have all three.

You can have superior service *and* low price while still, paradoxically, making more money than anybody else. This is accomplished by having the right mix of business, a combination where the amount of money-making business far outweighs the money-losing business across all sectors and product lines.

Any company that achieves this combination will run their business at a profit rate two to three times that of industry, association, and market averages. This is absolutely possible and any business can do it.

Our research has found that distributors can reduce the margins on their best customers by between 500 and 800 basis points (margin reductions between five and eight percent) while still keeping the accounts very profitable. (Your mileage may vary.)

There's been some controversy over my suggestion that companies could go to their customers and start to unilaterally offer lower pricing on the products they carry.

The countervailing logic comes from the environment we've been stuck in for a while now, where margins are believed to be the direct path to profitability. However, the math has shown the argument is just simply wrong because gross margins aren't correlated to profitability in any meaningful way.

There's an instinct to always keep the prices up and never discount. It's certainly not a bad strategy when you have a good working relationship where the customer is satisfied, you're satisfied, and the relationship isn't at risk. Under this scenario, there's not much point in lowering price, especially if you're making extraordinary profits.

However, if you want to more deeply penetrate the accounts, give customers access to additional opportunities where special things come along, and you already have a very profitable regime, then this will give you the ability to capitalize on those opportunities.

Use Service & Price to Acquire Target HVAs

When you've completed the earlier steps, your company is generating increased $GP, but has fewer PDAs siphoning profits. Newly acquired HVAs and HPAs and used-to-be PDAs are consuming less of your infrastructure costs leaving you with additional bottom line.

Since your HVA profits are subsidizing losses from a much smaller cadre of PDAs, you have cash flow available to aggressively price target HVAs.

In trying to acquire a new account, most reps have little tangible to offer. Absent a relationship-disrupting event on the other side, the rep is usually forced to rely in rapport- and relationship-building to persuade the account to switch.

High-Potential Accounts											
	Customer	Revenue	GP			Exp		NBC		Invoices	Type
		$	$	%	/inv	$	%	$	%	Total	
1	Medical Life Insurance Co	153,433	55,899	36.4%	451	31,898	20.8%	24,001	15.6%	124	HVA
5	Telstar International Inc	54,713	17,336	31.7%	403	12,221	22.3%	5,115	9.3%	43	HPA
6	Millennium Bostonian Hotel	261,580	43,161	16.5%	389	38,305	14.6%	4,856	1.9%	111	HVA
7	Riggs Distler & Company Inc	25,668	16,607	64.7%	353	11,922	46.4%	4,685	18.3%	47	HPA
8	Richardson Myers & Donofrio	43,143	12,807	29.7%	610	8,126	18.8%	4,680	10.8%	21	HVA
19	Premier Farnell	13,462	8,619	64.0%	137	9,115	67.7%	(496)	(3.7%)	63	PDA
20	Stokes Merrill Inc	264,814	55,441	20.9%	402	56,213	21.2%	(771)	(0.3%)	138	PDA

figure 10.01—using HVA metrics to price target HVAs

Account acquisition is a lot more likely if the rep can offer good business justifications for the move, and now concierge service and aggressive pricing are available.

A good place to get guidance on price is from the existing business. In approaching an account like #8: Richardson Myers, I can pull several useful metrics:

- $43,000 revenue on 21 invoices = ~$2,000 / invoice
- 29.7% GM% and 18.8% Exp%

Working from this, I can attempt to "buy" the account with a proposal the looks something like:

- 25% GM% (about 5% under market price)
- orders must be $2,000 minimum
- invoices paid in 30days
- two no-charge shipments per month (other pay normal rates)
- access to our Platinum Service team

This gives target accounts several business reasons to try our company, and produces large enough orders to ensure they'll be an HVA.

The business may be less profitable than our model account, but will add profit and cash flow to the company.

For instance, you could have your salesperson say, "We really want you to try out the great service at our company. To prove that we're the best around, we're willing to provide you with special pricing for the first month (or first week or first order). Give us a shot at bring us your next big deal and we'll price it below the market average so you can see that we're able to live up to our promises."

This helps the sales force by giving them a selling point more compelling than trying to merely sell on the basis of rapport building and promises. They're giving the buyer a chance to test your company with pricing that screams, "You have to try this out!" Once you get them to give you a try, it's a lot easier to grab all of their business and then start working on penetration.

Meanwhile, the incumbent supplier's margin-protection policies will make him unwilling to match your pricing. Without an advanced understanding of profit generation, he'll also view the target as a midsized account, and is unlikely to work aggressively to protect it.

The competition's limiting beliefs will work in your favor, leaving them helpless to counter your strategy.

The Lost Art of Negotiation

Efforts to manage and control selling have largely taken true negotiation out of the process. For the most part, selling has devolved to: customer wants a product; sales "negotiates" the price.

You cannot successfully negotiate on a single dimension.

For instance, you want to sell for $10 and the customer wants to pay $8. You compromise at $9, and neither side gets what they need. Next time, the customer still wants $8, and you compromise at $8.50. Again, neither side gets what it needs, and the price is continually ratcheted down.

This has been going on for years and tends to squeeze margins out of the business.

Top selling organizations have a multi-dimensional approach, and this means bringing in the transactions that drive CTS.

For instance, Amazon has a multi-dimensional negotiation embodied in its system.

I can assemble and order, and then I have a range of delivery options, each with its own price. I can get the order delivered same day for $34; tomorrow for $18; later this week (by mail) for $8, or whenever they can conveniently put it on a truck already passing my door for free.

This is brilliant! I can prioritize price or delivery speed to suit my needs, and Amazon has a mechanism to collect additional $GP to cover higher cost options.

The mistake we make is in fixing the price before we consider the terms, eliminating the opportunity for a multi-dimensional negotiation.

Takeaway: Develop a price policy that contemplates trading price levels for transaction count reductions. Train the sales force so they become good at using it to increase account profit when reducing margins.

Lock HVAs with Service & Price

You will already have extended your concierge service to your HVAs, and that program will help protect them against loss.

As your company is now generating higher profit rates, you can consider adjusting pricing for your existing accounts to a more aggressive level.

I'm not suggesting an across-the-board reduction unless there's a significant and compelling benefit for doing so.

However, you can certainly be ready to reprice accounts in some common circumstances:

- ✓ you can help an HVA win important business by providing special pricing to support the bid
- ✓ you have a competitive threat on an important HVA
- ✓ you have certain HVAs with expense rates well below the norm—a gold mine for you, or for a competitor that might get them—and you unilaterally reduce margin to protect the account (I'd suggest you tie the reduction to continued low transaction counts so the account does creep out of HVA status)

Another situation where you might consider adjusting your pricing involves being in a competitive market. If your competitors are taking the same approach as your company, in that they're actively attempting to acquire their best accounts' direct competition, then your best accounts may be at risk and lower pricing could help protect that relationship.

Using Price for Account Penetration

Pricing should also be considered when trying for deeper account penetration. Unless your salesperson has incredible insights into the customer—which is very rare—there's no good way of knowing whether you're getting all of that account's business.

Many companies spread or split their business. They usually wind up buying products from other suppliers because they don't know you carry the product. Using more aggressive tactics to convince them increase their order sizes, which increases your profits since the gross profit goes up while the logistical costs remain around the same, is one way around this issue.

For example, if your customer buys product lines A and B from you but they also have a need for C, which they currently get from somebody else, you can price the C price at a special rate to get them into the fold.

Another example might be a very large bid where the pricing would need to be, or should be, lower than their regular pricing due to the significant volumes of particular products involved in the bid. In that instance, there's no reason why you couldn't approach the customer and explain, "Because of our close partnership, we want to give you a unique opportunity. Let's team up and work out a special deal on a one-time basis because we think that we can help you get this deal." This upfront and honest approach can help you win the business and perhaps even improve your customer's loyalty.

As long as you're properly accounting for the logistical cost (or cost-to-serve) that comes with that particular sale or deal, it can still be a very profitable transaction. The fact the pricing is different or lower than the norm won't impact that profitability. It's a good deal for both companies.

Takeaway: Develop policies the sales reps can use to trade price decreases for incremental business.

Ensure HVAs remain HVAs

When you have benefits directly tied to HVA status, you also need monitoring to identify situations where HVAs drop back to an HPA or even PDA status.

In addition, you'll need a process to get them back into HVA, or a mechanism to adjust or withdraw the benefits.

If you have an account that runs its business efficiently, I would suggest that you provide yourself with a certain amount of insurance against that account wandering away by offering conditional pricing. You can explain to the customer they're working with you in a very efficient manner and producing good volume at a very low logistical cost. As long as they continue to do so, you can give them more attractive pricing.

Takeaway: Your company needs a monitoring mechanism to spot HVAs that change into HPAs or PDAs, and a method to help them get back to the HVA status.

Summary

In conclusion, you stand to gain a substantial pricing advantage by shifting some of the excess or extraordinary profits acquired from your platinum accounts away from subsidizing your money-losing accounts. The dollars you free up can then be used for marketing or pricing purposes to help acquire new accounts and penetrate existing ones.

You're not losing anything in the process because this pricing model or pricing advantage is funded by a reduction in losses on the money-losing side of the ledger. Your bottom line ultimately remains unchanged. The only difference is the money is now being put to good use where it's working to grow your business, your volume, your reach, your penetration and, most importantly, your profit so your bottom line can grow even further.

Step 6: Managing the Trading Process

In earlier chapters, you learned about implementing concierge-level customer service. You learned policies and practices that would target your sales efforts and activities on accounts to make them more profitable. I then discussed how large service drain accounts could be converted into profitable accounts and, by this time, you should have some progress on those ideas. This helped you get ready to start having some of those larger money-losing accounts leave because you had produced new of gross profit elsewhere, giving you the financial ability give up some of the money-losing gross profit producers at the bottom of your customer list.

These changes should put you in a position to actively manage the trading process. This means you're at the point when you can actively do things to drive away accounts which can't be converted into money-makers (or likely will never be money-makers). The goal is to send these accounts straight into the waiting arms of the competition.

This is where you really begin to move your company into profit-performance territory, where others just can’t keep up, and your whale curve is becoming highly optimized for profit.

Your company also is consolidating what it does in a winning new culture of profit-driven attitudes, processes and incentives.

Trading Away PDAs

In prior parts of the strategy, there's been an effort to work with PDAs to improve the relationship from where your business is exploited into more of a "win-win" where there's a mutual benefit.

There will be certain accounts which cannot, or will not, allow changes that lead to a better relationship, leaving your company actually paying them to be a customer.

For these accounts, it will be necessary to begin a process which will force the issue, by first implementing policies which will provide new $GP to reduce the losses they're driving, or to encourage the account to switch to a competitor.

It's important that everyone on your team—especially in sales—understands and is in support of this if it becomes necessary. Quantifying the scale of the loss driven by the account is a very helpful tool for this.

Managing the trading process is more about attitude and timing than anything else. Timing is important because you can't drive off big accounts without first replacing the gross profit from somewhere else, such as through reforming or adding other accounts.

Attitude is important because you're attempting to overcome years or decades of tradition where every sale was thought to be a good sale. You're battling against commonly held beliefs like, "If gross profit is coming in, you must be making money on it somehow," and, "Their costs can't be as high as you think they are." Of course, you know better than that because, in the wholesale distribution business, more than 60% of all invoices lose money and a great deal of those come from large scale accounts which have too many invoices for the unit of gross profit.

Just as you came to understand and believe these ideas, you have to make sure that your team understands them as well. Your salespeople need to understand these accounts aren't healthy for anybody to have, especially not your company.

Going through the management process where you cultivate this understanding may be particularly difficult. In many cases, it goes against everything they know and have practiced for decades. They'll likely worry that you've made a mistake because it's so unusual for a company to turn down business. In fact, it's almost unheard of for their company to turn down business of any sort... and it's precisely what gave your company serious profit and cash flow issues in the first place!

Remember: If you don't say "No" to anything, you don't have a strategy. Strategies are made up of not only what you do, but also what you consciously choose not to do. One of the things you should be consciously not be doing is accepting business from accounts where you cannot possibly make money. These accounts can only take away some of the profit you've already made.

I've been in meetings before where this concept confused attendees. It made them very skeptical and they thought I was wrong for recommending it. I recall one very senior sales manager asking, "Are you telling me I have to get rid of my best accounts?" He clearly didn't understand the paradigm shift the company was trying to implement.

Perhaps a little less than diplomatically, my response was, "These aren't *best* accounts. These are blood-sucking vampires that jumped on the neck of your territory and are draining the life blood from it. No matter how big these vampires are, they aren't good for you. If you don't prevent them from draining those profits, your branch will die."

It was imperative for the sales manager to recognize these weren't good accounts. They weren't even okay accounts. They were accounts which actively depleted his ability to make money at the branch. By letting these accounts operate in the way they had, he was preventing the branch from being extremely profitable.

To drive this point home for the sales manager, we went through the numbers associated with one of the accounts. We saw how much drain there was and what the branch would look like if it instead had another account, one which wasn't half as large, but also didn't have all of the logistical or operational costs that profit-draining accounts drove. We then looked at how another profitable account could be served with the time and costs freed up by not having the original.

Thanks to this demonstration, the manager began to recognize the reasoning and the benefit of not having this particular account. A more aggressive manager might have also quickly recognized the benefit of this money-losing account being in the hands of the competition where it would consume their resources, waste their time, drain their profits, remove their ability to hire, stop them from expanding their lines, limit their service, and do other harms.

Make no mistake: This account was causing the branch significant harm. It wasn't just preventing them from being able to grow their capabilities, it was forcing them to shrink those capabilities. They couldn't afford the customer service people anymore. They couldn't afford the free deliveries anymore. They couldn't afford other services as well, because they had too many of these accounts coming in.

It's only a matter of time before accounts like these have no place to hide. Eventually everybody will recognize that doing business with these accounts, in the way the accounts want to do business, is dysfunctional and unprofitable.

Distributors will be unwilling to do business with accounts on those bases as well. When nobody is willing to work with them, the accounts will be forced to conduct themselves in a business-like manner which will provide a win-win for both sides. However, that's not the case today and, until things change, you can use this reality to your advantage.

Takeaway: Be sure the sales team understands the rationale and profit benefits of losing a PDA. Cultivate an attitude where all customers are welcome as long as they're part of a win-win.

Driving Off PDAs

This brings us to the accounts which can't be converted. Before anything else can be done with these accounts, you need to establish a mindset among your employees that it's okay for these accounts to go away and losing them will actually be a good thing. It may take some time and effort to overcome the resistance to this idea because the notion will be counter-intuitive to some of your salespeople.

Although it's intended that unreformable PDAs will go to competitors, it's a bad idea to convey a message to an account that you want them gone.

For this reason, I'd caution against using the stronger language from this book—it'll likely be picked up by your team members and will inevitably be heard by customers in the marketplace. (I use it here so my attitude toward customers that drain profits is unambiguous, and no one has the opportunity to argue I have a positive view of what PDAs do to your profits.)

You *never* want to deliver a message that says a customer is unwelcome. Instead, you'd like to seem friendly and available—for every customer willing to be part of a win-win relationship.

The act of getting PDAs to leave should be through policies, procedures, fees and exceptions that favor HVAs and add $GP to PDAs.

Some of these might be:

- ✓ higher margin in pricing guidelines (adds $GP and creates pricing differential for HVAs)
- ✓ strict credit compliance: account goes on hold at 30 days (improves A/R turns and reduces write-off risk)
- ✓ no sales representation (reduces compensation costs)
- ✓ no free samples (reduces inventory costs)
- ✓ all deliveries are billed to customer (adds $GP)
- ✓ billing services (i.e. multi-billing for product delivered to single address) are broken out and charged (adds $GP)
- ✓ special stock orders carry a procurement charge (adds $GP)

Adding fees is a good way to either: raise $GP to make business more profitable, or give the customer a choice between a fee to cover requested special services or a behavior change to avoid them.

If a PDA decides to defect to a competitor, then break out the champagne!

You want to actively build on that structure and reinforce those kinds of policies. Luckily, there are many things you can do on this front. By actively managing and aggressively encouraging your sales force to bring in big wins for serviceable accounts, you can start to bring pricing into the equation, which is something which will be covered in greater detail in the next chapter.

Takeaway: Use policies, pricing and fees to first change behavior and profitability, or to create a motivation for a PDA to leave of his own volition. Never drive off an account directly.

Playing Hardball

As a last ditch effort, your salespeople can make one final call on these accounts to let them know your company is really trying to make the relationship work. However, these accounts need to put in some effort as well. If they insist on maintaining the status quo, then they can go. For instance, if you're adding delivery fees and they refuse to pay them, then they go on credit hold. And, of course, there will be no free samples and other perks.

You're taking this strong-arm approach because the accounts are de facto unreformable and the real goal is to convince them to do business with somebody else. Of course, the competition might also be unwilling to do business in the way these accounts demand.

In most cases, your competitors won't be smart enough to refuse these unreformable, profit-draining accounts. These competitors will quickly find themselves mystified by the fact they have all of this new business yet they're somehow making less money. They won't know what you do about profit strategy and, thanks to their limiting beliefs, they're going to defeat themselves.

Trading Checklist

Your company is ready to actively manage trading when it has these important elements in place:

- ✓ concierge customer service team
- ✓ training on concierge service for the sales team
- ✓ identification of HPAs / HVAs / PDAs
- ✓ sales and concierge service are teamed up and working together on HVAs and HPAs
- ✓ you've already reduced CTS on some PDAs, moving them into HPA or HVA status
- ✓ sales team has identified and is targeting potential new HVAs
- ✓ you've already added replacement $GP with new HVAs and HPAs
- ✓ company has systems and incentives to prevent adding new PDAs
- ✓ you have pricing and service policies designed to drive $GP add-ons for PDAs to reduce losses or change behavior
- ✓ you've built a positive feedback system to recognize and reinforce the dropping of PDAs

Summary

In conclusion, once you have the most important pins in place, it's time to begin managing the trading process. This is a two-way process where you’re just not only bringing in new accounts you're actively working to move the unfixable accounts out. Those accounts will hopefully wind up in the hands of your competitors and burden them enough that you can steal their best.

With concierge-level customer service, your salespeople will also have a real business-based story to tell prospects and new customers. They'll also be armed with a great target list which they've built by performing a thorough analysis. The list will include your best accounts' direct competitors, who most likely are among your competitors' best accounts, and by gaining their business you're likely to devastate your competition at the same time.

If you're doing everything right, you'll see some drastic changes in your company's whale curve. The peak internal profit at the top of your whale curve will increase while the tail end decreases because the service drain accounts which were dragging you down have been converted into profitable accounts which are giving your company a boost.

Step 7: Business Models

Most of the strategy so far has been focused on the HPAs that individually drive the scale and shape of your profit whale curves, because that's where it's easiest and fastest to leverage your profit.

There's usually a pretty good secondary opportunity in the balance of the business, if you take a more strategic view.

This comes from thinking about the business models your company employs to present, sell and monetize its products and service to its customers.

What's a Business Model?

A business model (or, service model, as I've also referred to it) is a way of encompassing all the things you do to accommodate the business you get from a certain type of customer or for a certain type of offering. (For instance: government sales; rentals; schools; design services; counter sales; etc.)

In maybe the best book on the topic, Business Model Generation (ISBN: 978-0470-87641-1), authors Osterwalder and Pignuer state, "A business model describes the rationale of how an organization creates, delivers and captures value."

Most companies are created to make money doing one thing, using a model copied from elsewhere, and then grow into what they are by responding to the market and copying what they observe around them. Adding, perhaps, a few innovations of their own, they use their initial and central model for everything they do.

Operating without a properly thought-out business model is almost always wasteful of resources and manpower, and can make certain parts of the business completely dysfunctional.

If you have a chronically-unprofitable business unit, it's most likely operating with a business model unsuited to its purpose. It's probable the unit could be made profitable by having a proper business model, or it could be the unit simply cannot be profitable because there's no rational model for it—something that could be discovered in about 90 minutes by putting it through the modelling process described in the book.

Takeaway: Chronically-dysfunctional business units are usually operating without a complete or planned business model. Creating a specific model can fill the missing gaps that cause losses.

Importance of Tailored Business Models

There are nine elements required of any functional model, and without any one of them the unit cannot function profitably.

It's not my intent to teach modelling here—I'll leave that for the aforementioned book, but suffice it to say every business unit, or type of business your company does will be well served if you take time to create and maintain an individual model for it.

Marginal Accounts

Much of the focus thus far has been on large, high volume accounts. However, there's another program that can be used to change the nature of the profitability of your business that runs parallel to the large volume account program.

When you look at your average and small accounts, you're going to find you make good money on a number of mid-velocity accounts. These accounts will serve as a model for the activities you'll want to do more of, because they can sustain the middle part of your business.

At the low end of the business, where the gross profit dollars are extremely small on an account-by-account or invoice-by-invoice basis, it's very difficult to make money. Your company would be well-served if it evaluated whether or not you should be involved in this kind of business. If you decide to keep those small accounts, you should strongly consider developing a separate service model for them.

There's a general trend in most companies where they started off with a model designed to service accounts at a certain level but, as they grew, they acquired increasingly larger customers and adapted accordingly. This includes providing more services, facilities, EDI trade credits, delivery, and all kinds of resources that develop in a natural wholesale distribution environment. That model, which evolved and grew over time to be better-suited to large accounts, is then applied to the entire customer base.

This process is the opposite of segmentation, which is something most companies understand they should be doing.

The purpose of segmentation isn't merely to identify the different groupings of customers, but it also serves as a management tool to help companies design specific service models for similar customers in those groups.

When you look at those groups, you'll find some small-fry accounts at the bottom. These are customers who generate $1,000, $500, or even as little as $200 of gross profit per year and, quite frankly, could never be serviced on a profitable basis under your company's traditional model.

Therefore, if you want to retain those accounts, you're going to need a different model so you can service them profitability. The first step in developing a model for those service accounts, after identifying who they are, is to start looking at your P&L statement. Your P&L contains every expense or every significant expense the company encounters in providing its products and services to its customer base.

Start by examining each line item to determine if the service is necessary for those accounts. For necessary services, is it an expense the customer would be willing to pay for? If it's either unnecessary or the customer won't pay for it, it's best for the company to find some way to forego the service.

For instance, if you have an account generating three invoices per year, adding up to about $200, does it make sense to set them up in the accounts receivable system? Does it make sense to create a trade account for them so you can send them a bill 30 days later which they probably won't pay so you'll have to collect 90 days later, forcing you to hire people to handle collections because you have of all these small invoices? The answer is "No."

If you have a counter sales operation, don't bother extending trade credits to small accounts which just wander in off the street. Those are policies created for larger, true wholesale customers who frequently buy in large volumes and consume enough products over the course of a year to justify paying an accounts receivable person to collect the money. Instead, have those small accounts pay on the spot with a check or credit card.

On that same note, even if you have a free delivery policy, does it make sense to apply free delivery to customers whose gross profit numbers for the entire year are incapable of covering the expense for the free delivery? The answer is "No."

These small accounts shouldn't qualify for free delivery. You can establish a lot of barriers (including some reasoning for the policy) so everybody, including the customer, will understand you don't offer free delivery to accounts which do less than $1,000 a year. Or, you don't offer free delivery on orders under $200. Or, you don't offer free delivery on the second order in the day.

There are a lot of things that you can do to change the service model, but you also really need to look at all of the items on the P&L statement.

How about the warehouse expense? Counter sales in wholesale distribution is almost a universal money loser. It's usually a significant drain because it's a model which involves pulling people away from doing the pick-pack-and-ship operation for large accounts.

When somebody walks in the door, these workers have to go man the register. Usually the customer will ask them for advice and talk to them for a few minutes. Then the worker is sent to the racks for an item or very small volume of product which still needs to be processed as a sale.

Meanwhile, the employee isn't getting work done for the important accounts—the customers who keep the business running—because they're too busy chasing tiny orders which pop up at random intervals.

What you have is your company's highest paid and most expensive product preparation resource being consumed by very small customers who aren't even buying enough products to cover the cost of the counter person. It's the epitome of dysfunctional business!

A lot of companies have solved this problem by converting their counter sales into a mini retail operation. They stock the most commonly purchased counter items in bins and racks in front of the counter area so customers can do their own picks. These customers can find whatever they need, much like they would at Home Depot and Costco, and then come up front to purchase it.

Some particularly ambitious companies have even implemented their own automated self-checkout lanes like you see at grocery stores and certain retailers. This allows customers to scan their own products and process their own transaction, right down to paying at the end. This ensures that very little man-power is wasted on these smaller customers. It's an ideal method for companies that want to incorporate counter sales into their strategy.

To sum things up, it's vital that you create new service models for accounts which don't fit your company's regular model. This can help to turn some smaller accounts which usually detract from the bottom line into contributors. However, even if you only wind up cutting your losses, you're still going to be much better off than you are today.

> Takeaway: Small accounts almost certainly need an independent business model tailored for their size and needs. Taking time to create a fully-planned model can make this whole category a profit contributor to your company.

Strategy End-State

The purpose of every strategy is to articulate a path and methodology for reaching an important objective.

The culmination of implementing the strategy here is to create a culture and practice that's focused on accumulating the bulk of a market's High-Value- and High-Potential Accounts by delivering a superior customer experience and aggressive, but targeted, pricing.

The company should be the most profitable of its peer group, producing profit rates at least two to three times industry averages.

The company should be, or have a realistic pathway to be, debt-free. It will also have the wherewithal to acquire other less-capable companies to fuel growth.

Perhaps most importantly, it should help all its stakeholders meet or exceed their own goals.

A good short-list for your company's post-strategy state might look like:

- ✓ Profits 2x-3x Industry Norms
- ✓ Debt-Free (Including Credit Line)
- ✓ Accelerate Growth Through Acquisition
- ✓ Above Average Pay for Contributors
- ✓ Best Place to Work

Conclusion

The strategy elements in this book have proven effective and productive for some of the pioneering companies of the new millennium. Using the advanced costing and profit monitoring systems like WayPoint Analytics, they've escaped the false indicators of Gross Margin and past practices to embrace and inculcate profit-driven strategies and practices.

Shaking off the conventional wisdom of the last century, they're setting new records while becoming the new dominant players.

As you move to adopt the same winning strategies, your organization can easily maintain and enhance your market position.

As you've seen in the book, failure to move into the new regime has major risks—when a competitor begins to trade best and worst accounts to his own benefit, there's a very short window before your company loses the ability to counter.

It's my hope the information in this book will help you change the profit performance and market position of your company in profoundly positive ways.

Bonus Chapter: Understanding Profit Drivers

This chapter comes from my book: Using Analytics to Manage Profit and is critical to anyone wanting a deeper understanding of how profits are created and lost so they can actively control the results they're responsible for.

This chapter is crucial, as it lays out the underlying business dynamics that directly control profit. Building on these dynamics, I create a profit strategy the profit-driven plan will directly support.

Working back from the end-state is always helpful in developing an effective path to a goal.

Obviously, the desired end-state is to have the company drive much-above-average profits and cash flow. To accomplish this, the company will have to shift focus and activities toward those customers most likely to produce profits, and away from those that produce losses. It will adopt strategies and processes to support this goal, and those reps making the best contributions will be well rewarded.

A deep and detailed understanding of what, precisely, creates incremental profits and incremental losses in the company's operations is crucial to the development of any successful profit-generating strategy.

Some of the surprising insights in this section provide clarity of purpose and a direct path to eradicating the profit-destroying traditions and practices of below-average companies.

Understanding real profit mechanics and the analytics required to monitor and manage them is key to designing, implementing and maintaining an effective pay plan.

Why Accounting Systems Can't Provide Profit Information

The accounting systems used in virtually all companies are completely unable to help manage profit. In fact, the core functional mechanics of accounting systems confound our ability to understand profits.

This is because they were designed to aggregate sales and costs into a single bottom line number. Their principle functions are to manage inventory, manage receivables, and produce a single bottom line number for banking and tax purposes.

A specialized companion system that calculates granular costs and profits is required to develop good profit strategies, and to track and manage profits.

> Takeaway: Your accounting system cannot produce granular profit numbers sufficient to support analysis, strategy, tactics or monitoring of profit-driving activities.

How Money is Made — Really

I'll preface the discussion with the most important aspects of the profit generation mechanics of a business, and the overall objective of every profit strategy.

I also need to introduce the vernacular of profit strategy used throughout the book. (See the Glossary for a complete list.)

The base mechanism of profit generation is bringing in Gross Profit (GP) and performing the functions the customer is paying for with a lower Cost-to-Serve (CTS), leaving a profit (Net Before Taxes or NBT).

	Rev (revenue)
–	COGS (Cost of Goods Sold)
=	GP (gross profit)
–	CTS (Cost-To-Serve)
=	NBT (Net Before Taxes)

figure 1.1—Traditional P&L

The Most Critical Understanding of Profit

Building on this basic structure creates a way to clearly understand the profit dynamics of every enterprise, and creates a framework for solid profit management.

Each sale produces a Gross Profit—the amount left from the revenue after the product is paid for. GP is actually the operating budget for the sale. You can't spend any more than the GP amount on operating expenses (and sales compensation), or the sale will generate a loss.

This is a core concept for all profit strategies.

Now for the interesting part—most sales, in every business, carry a CTS that exceeds the GP! In wholesale distribution, the median percentage of money-losing invoices is 62.5%. This means more than half of all sales in a typical distribution business lose money!

More surprisingly, those companies that get the money-losing proportion below 50% generate outstanding profit rates—usually 2x or 3x the industry average!

Accounting systems lead most executives to a core belief that every sale meeting a minimum Gross Margin (GM%) threshold makes some additive contribution to the bottom line. This is completely false, yet drives a zeal to get every sale possible, leading most companies to mediocre profit generation (at best).

Analysis shows absolutely no correlation between GM% and profitability. Belief to the contrary is the most debilitating factor in business, and is directly contributory to nearly every dysfunctional practice and initiative.

Takeaway: Gross Margin % has no correlation to actual profit, and is being replaced with NBC for effective analysis and management of profitability.

This erroneous belief is incompatible with any kind of strategy for superior profit performance, and its widespread existence is why the vast majority of companies languish at profit levels at or below the average.

figure 1.2—Spread

Every productive profit strategy will, in effect, aim to properly balance GP production with CTS consumption, and to drive increases in the spread between these two elements.

Takeaway: Every sale has its own profit-production mechanics. Most sales will tend to produce a loss that consumes profits already made elsewhere. Recognizing and acting on this is key to nearly every profit-oriented strategy or practice.

Net Before Compensation

A new metric vital to useful profit strategies and for profit-based pay systems is Net Before Compensation (NBC). NBC is created by excluding customer-facing sales rep pay from operating expenses, and having a sub-total indicating the profit generated before the reps are paid. (figure 1.3)

This is critical to profit-based pay schemes because it creates a reliable profit number on which to base pay calculations. (It eliminates the circular calculation issue that occurs if the sales pay is, itself, part of the profit total driving the pay.)

	Revenue
–	COGS (Cost of Goods Sold)
=	GP (Gross Profit)
–	CTS (Cost-To-Serve or operating expenses)
=	**NBC (Net Before Sales Compensation)**
–	Sales Comp
=	NBT (Net Before Taxes)

figure 1.3—Enhanced P&L

It also creates what is probably the most useful profit analysis metric yet invented. Because sales incentive pay is so widely variable—full of exceptions like draws and guarantees, special commission rates, etc.—including sales pay in profit analysis will confound nearly any practical numeric analysis. NBC solves this issue.

NBC is coming into wide use as a management metric because it encompasses the full spectrum of financial elements that affect profitability—volume, margins and operating expenses —into a single number.

Takeaway: NBC is the central metric of effective profit analysis and likely the best way to monitor and manage profit.

Customer Segmentation

Segmentation is a useful management tool to group customers with similar characteristics. This allows the development of tactics that can be applied to most or all of the members of the group.

For our purposes, it's useful to segment customers based on profitability. I'm most interested in the NBC profit production shown within the segments. This will be used later in the strategy development for the company.

Profit segmentation provides an understanding as to which companies (or proportion of the companies) generate the bulk of profitability within a territory, a product line, or the whole company.

For the purpose of illustration, I'm using a single sales territory where customers have been segmented by profitability and GP volume. You should immediately notice that roughly $81,000 of NBC comes from the "Core" group of just 16 customers (the block in the upper-right quadrant). These are major customers who not only bring in a lot of profit on each order, but also buy in great volume. They're customers who you'd wish you had more of.

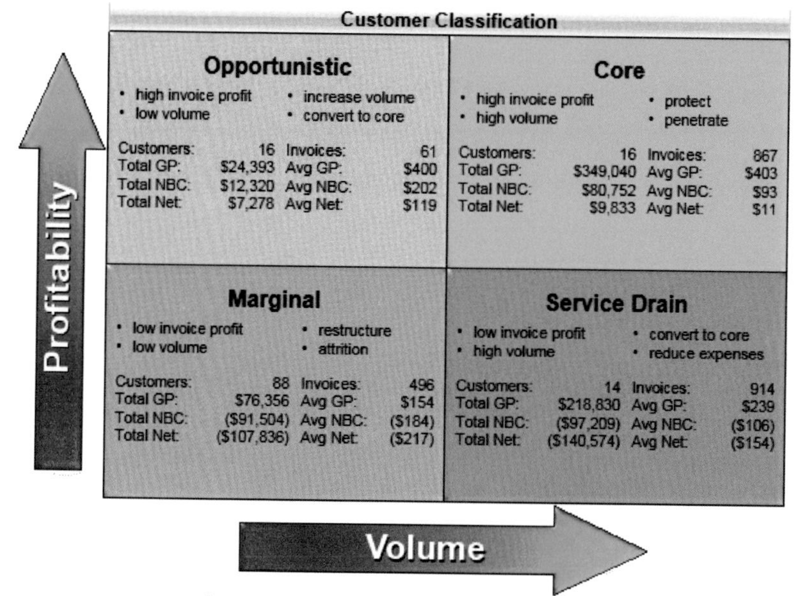

figure 1.4—Customer Segmentation by Profit Value

Strategically, you'd want to protect these accounts and deepen your penetration by finding more to sell to them. These accounts are best in the hands of reps who will work to serve them by preventing and correcting the inevitable issues found in high-volume relationships.

However, as you look at the other groupings, you'll notice that those quadrants aren't nearly as productive. There's an "Opportunistic" segment (upper left) that's bringing in another $12,000 NBC from 16 customers. It's good, but it's certainly not great. If you could get a lot more of their business, you'd be very happy.

The strategy here is to recognize them as a source for future growth, as this is where emerging accounts will be found, as well as large accounts which are giving the company only a portion of their business. This is where aggressive field sales pays off.

The other two segments are losers. The territory in this example is losing over $91,000 NBC doing business with the 88 small customers in the "Marginal" segment (lower left). There may be ways to turn things around and make some of them profitable, but currently, it's business that isn't delivering on profit, and the accounts here will likely never deliver significant volume.

These accounts are usually best as self-serve house accounts, served via web and telesales. Policy changes, pricing and GP add-ons are most commonly used to address this segment.

Finally, there's the "Service Drain" (lower right) segment where the company is losing roughly $97,000 NBC between fourteen large accounts who bring in a lot of highly unprofitable volume.

These are high-volume accounts, usually with logistical requirements that consume more resources than the GP can cover. The inefficiencies affect the customers' own profitability as well, but they may be unaware of it. They'll need some selling effort and perhaps some management attention to turn around.

Overall, this is a money-losing territory. The roughly $93,000 NBC from the profitable customers is being completely devoured by roughly $189,000 in losses. It's difficult, if not impossible, to compete with that kind of a handicap.

If you were to just look at the territory through the lens of typical accounting systems, you'd never notice that you have all of these great customers being dragged down by completely awful business from unprofitable clients.

Takeaway: Although there are many ways companies segment their customers, to do so on profit potential (GP), and profit production(NBC), is one of the most useful in profit analysis.

As a first principle, I'd like to make sure I'm not paying commissions to salespeople managing those massive money-sinks. The absolute last thing you want to do is pay to lose that much money. By not paying commissions on these profit-killing transactions, you'll not only see fewer bad orders but salespeople will start to pursue more profitable customers.

Whale Curves

A very important philosophical or analytical device is the "whale curve". It's a great tool for visualizing what's really going on with the profit-generating mechanics in your business.

The visual is the key to understanding the profit strategy I'll be developing shortly.

Whale curves are created by charting the accumulated profit from a profit ranking report. In figure 1.5, the curve ranks customers by profitability, starting in the lower left with zero, then adding the profit from the most profitable account, then stacking the addition profit from the second, third, fourth, fifth, and so on, until there are no more customers to list.

Zone 1 on the left shows customers who generate pretty fair amounts of profitability and put large increments of profits on the bottom line of the company. You can see that $5M of profit is coming in from less than 20% of the customers.

These are the customers that pay the proverbial freight for everything in the company. They allow the company to rack up huge losses elsewhere and still be profitable.

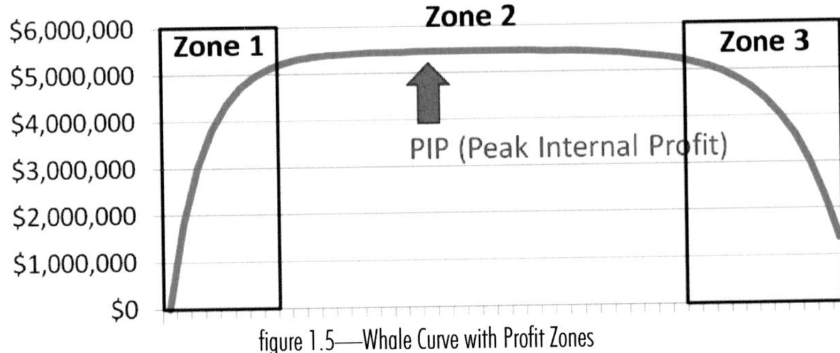

figure 1.5—Whale Curve with Profit Zones

Personally, I think it's unfair that your best customers are paying high prices and making high margins so you can afford do business with their competitors in a way that imposes all kinds of costs and drains profits. You certainly wouldn't want to go to a bank to borrow some money and just hand it to the customer, but this is what you're essentially doing by taking the profit from one customer to cover another customer's losses.

The thought of burdening your best and most efficient (read: low-CTS) customers by using their much-higher profits to cover the losses you take on their competitors should make you feel a little queasy. I think it's unacceptable. Not just on a moral level, but because it drives you to strategies that make your best accounts vulnerable to poaching by your competitors.

Zone 2 is the middle section making up the whale's "back" and consists of small accounts which make or lose a few dollars. These accounts are largely "noise" in the business, driving the need for much of the company's personnel and infrastructure, but producing little or no profit.

Getting to the bottom of the profit ranking, the customers that make up Zone 3 are significant accounts which are losing the company greater and greater amounts of money.

Through the lens of a typical accounting system, you'd see only the $1.3M bottom line for this company. The company president might be thinking to himself, "If you can get 15% more next year, taking the bottom line up to $1.5M, you'll post a great gain!" He'd be completely blind to the fact there's $5.5M of profit in the business already, but most of it is being lost to losses from a group of customers receiving far more resources and services than they actually pay for.

Takeaway: Every company has a whale curve, which will reveal the massive scale of unrealized profit. Just knowing how much profit is available is the first step to setting goals to capture it.

Changing this dynamic can almost instantly increase a company's profit by a huge increment.

For example, if the losses on the money-losing business were cut in half, the profit line in this business goes from $1.2M to $3.5M. That's more like a 200% gain! By doing nothing else, the company would triple its bottom line.

Experience shows the potential is actually much higher—large-volume money-losing accounts are those most easily and most quickly converted into significant money-makers. The high CTS levels are mirrored on the customer's operations as well, so profit-producing reductions in CTS immediately and automatically benefit the customer.

Most of the activity required to get this done will occur at the customer-contact surface of the business—the sales force. This is why a profit-driven incentive plan is so important—it synchronizes rep incentives and rewards with the company's desire to produce stellar profits.

Gross Profit Production

For centuries, while business was recorded on ledger sheets, revenue was the principle measure of scale and value of a customer.

Computer systems widely adopted in the 1980s gave most businesses the first convenient access to Gross Profit (GP) and Gross Margin (GM%), and these measures have come into more common usage.

For me, GP is a much more useful indicator of account scale and potential. It's a real number that accurately represents the operating budget for a territory, customer, or even an individual sale.

As the top half of the GP / CTS equation, it's the starting point for profit. It also encompasses the first three controllable elements affected by the sales force: volume; pricing/margin; and add-ons like delivery charges or service fees.

All of these elements can have a direct effect on the profit potential of a sale, and need to be considered in a pay incentive plan.

Cost-to-Serve

Profit on every sale is the result of a balance between the mechanics of Gross Profit (GP) production, and the logistical elements that drive Cost-to-Serve (CTS).

In a distribution business, CTS is directly driven by the logistical elements of the operation. In profit analytics, it's easy to quantify the CTS-driving transaction counts that occur in the flow of business.

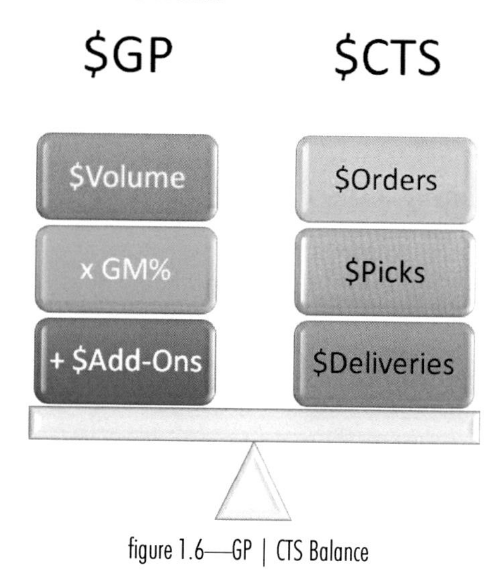

figure 1.6—GP | CTS Balance

These most commonly break down to: orders; picks; invoices; and deliveries. CTS directly scales with all of these elements because the more of any of them that have to be accommodated, the more personnel and infrastructure a company will require.

Managing transaction counts has a direct effect on costs, and is the central priority for companies seeking outstanding profit generation rates. Since this is largely invisible to organizations without advanced granular profit analytical systems, it's also the area of greatest opportunity for profit growth

The principle objective is to reduce CTS per unit of GP. This opens several new avenues for profit growth. Every industry has pretty much exhausted all opportunities for pricing and margin increases, and can get volume increases only through increased market share, leaving only add-ons as a fertile area for GP increases.

Takeaway: Cost-to-Serve (CTS) is directly driven by transaction counts and usually represents the greatest opportunity for profit growth.

However, CTS management has been little managed and offers broad opportunities for improvement.

Who Controls CTS?

One important principle of a good incentive mechanic, is that it must reflect an aspect of the customer interaction the sales rep can influence. Otherwise, the incentive will be ineffective.

In distribution, the argument that reps can't control costs has frequently been offered as a reason not to include cost-related elements in sales pay plans.

I strongly disagree with this line of thinking.

Of course reps directly control costs! No CEO hires additional personnel or adds infrastructure out of malice or boredom. This is done strictly as a response to the activity attached to the sales coming in.

Costs are directly driven by service models required by the accounts the reps bring in. For instance, accounts which insist on separate invoices / shipments for each department, or place multiple orders each day represent a cost structure less likely to be profitable, and these terms are (or should be) part the pricing of the deal in the purview of rep.

Consider these items:

4) CTS drivers are integral to the terms of the sale—how the product will be ordered and delivered. Logistical requirements are as much an element subject to influence of the rep as are product selection, pricing and payment terms.
5) Pay mechanics are primarily intended to scale pay to sale profit value—the incentive value of any mechanic is completely determined by the nature of the rep in exploiting it to increase their individual pay.

It's important for pay mechanics to be tied to cost drivers. This ties pay to the profit value of sales, and may provide an incentive for the sales force with the intention of influencing the cost drivers as a secondary benefit.

High-Value Accounts

Customers in the most profitable Core group will almost always be those with low CTS% rates (CTS / Revenue). Customers of this group buy significant volumes with a much lower number of transactions than the average.

Put another way, they're the ones with the highest GP / CTS.

Given the prevalent profit philosophy today, where inordinate value is placed on GM%, margins are defended at nearly all costs, pricing policy is unlikely to very closely reflect the true profit value of an account's CTS rate.

This results in an environment where the best organized and most efficient customers produce outsized profit, which are used to offset (subsidize) losses driven by their less-capable competitors, which you also serve. In practice, this could be accurately described as in the following theoretical conversation:

> **Customer:** you need help with more aggressive pricing so you can pursue a great opportunity for both of us.
>
> **Sales Rep:** Oh, no—you can't do that. Although you make more money on you than any other account, you give the excess profits to your competition, who're so dysfunctional you couldn't even afford to service them without your help.

Although no sane person would actually convey this, it's reflective of the actual practice in most companies.

In a saturated market, the strategy of most players is to flog the sales force to bring in every account and sale they can get. With a strategy guaranteed to load the company with CTS that's driven by marginal and service drain accounts, their very survival is dependent on top accounts providing the profits required to subsidize the money-losing bulk of the business.

A much better plan is to shift priorities and resources away from the profit-drain accounts, shifting any that cannot be reformed to competitors, loading them with the boat anchors which will paralyze their ability to serve best accounts.

Meanwhile you have more resources to give concierge service to top accounts.

Losing the loss-subsidizing requirements of drain accounts allows better pricing for top accounts *without sacrificing profits.* Meanwhile, competitors loaded with more dysfunctional accounts are spread thin, and have even less ability to reach lower pricing levels to win back top accounts.

> Takeaway: A core recognition and identification of customer profit value opens the gateway to an intelligent and strategic process of trading off money losing customers to competitors, while going after their best accounts.

This process is a carefully managed version of the normal customer trading process every company has always engaged in with its competitors. The big difference is recognition of customer profit value and trading wisely.

Fully executed, this can have a devastating effect on competitors still grasping for every sale.

Profit Strategy—10,000-Foot View

Working from the information I've gathered, I know the following about profit drivers:

- ✓ Most sales add a loss to the bottom line and shifting the usual 65/35 loss/profit balance to a more favorable mix will significantly change the company's profit picture.
- ✓ GM% is unreliable for profit analysis and management, and should be replaced with NBC%.
- ✓ The company has sales that fall into three profit-affecting zones: significant profit producers; break-even noise and activity generators; and significant money-losers (whale curve).
- ✓ Customers fall into the four quadrants that indicate both their value to the company and the strategies for optimizing profit (customer segmentation).

Profit Strategy

This brings me to the most important central objective of the company's strategy. In its end-state, the sales force is working to draw in the most efficient and most profitable accounts, and these will almost always be those with a lower-than-average cost structure, and which are quite profitable at lower-than-average margin rates.

To be clear, high-efficiency accounts can operate at lower pricing and margin levels than is traditionally the case—*as long as the company no longer needs the additional profit to subsidize money-losing business at the other end of the whale curve.*

In this circumstance, the high-efficiency accounts can be attracted and defended with much more aggressive pricing. Our research estimates margins can typically be reduced by 8%-10% (your mileage may vary), while delivering the same or a higher bottom line for the company—*but only if the company eliminates enough of the money-losing business that's currently consuming the profits generated by the higher margins.*

A profit-driven sales compensation plan is a vital tool for accomplishing this fundamental strategy.

Execution: Tactics Implementing Strategy

Articulating my strategy for each element of my analysis helps bring focus to the important objectives which will later drive the elements of the sales compensation plan.

Core Accounts / Most Profitable

Protecting core accounts (accounts from the left end of the whale curve) is the first item on the list for any profit strategy. You want to shift resources and services toward these accounts so you can truly deliver superior service in every aspect of their interactions. This is through the entire range: answering their calls first; first priority on call-backs; first call on product; heroic rescues; service guarantees; favored pricing; etc.

These will be accounts with lower CTS rates, almost always buying with more product (read: GP) per transaction unit (order / pick / invoice / shipment). Find the markers common in these accounts, and then identify every account in the market likely to be similar and focus on bringing them in.

Service Drain Accounts / Most Unprofitable

The second item in a profit strategy action plan is to correct the dysfunction in the service drain accounts (those on the right end of the whale curve). These are always large accounts with some mechanism that drives up costs.

The cost-driving mechanism may be accidental and can be corrected, putting the account into the core group. If the cost-driver is inherent in the service model of the account itself (big box stores are commonly in this group), you can either shift the logistics back to the customer, or cede the account to your competition, loading them with a money-loser which will reduce their ability to compete on good accounts.

Marginal Accounts

Marginal accounts (the back of the whale curve) are relatively easy to fix with policy changes. The object is to use a combination of service cost reductions (removing commissions, A/R costs, counter costs), and add-ons (small-order fees, delivery markups, a-la-carte service fees) to either make them profitable through increased GP, or to encourage them to defect and drain the resources and profits of your competitors.

Glossary

CoGS—Cost of Goods Sold: purchase cost of product sold to customer as it appears above the Gross Profit line on a P&L statement (may include cost modifiers such as inbound freight and vendor rebates)

CTS—Cost to Serve: total of all operating expenses, excluding: rep-level sales compensation, extraordinary items, and usually non-cash expenses like depreciation

CTS%—percentage of revenue consumed by CTS (CTS ÷ revenue)

Delta—difference in results (usually profit) from one time period to another (usually year-over-year same period)

GM%—Gross Margin: the percentage of revenue represented by GP (GP ÷ revenue x 100)

GP—Gross Profit: fraction of revenue remaining after CoGS is deducted (revenue—CoGS)

HPA—High-Potential Account: accounts with above-average Gross Profit dollar generation. HPAs have the potential to be very large money-makers or very large money-losers. (You can't make (or lose) a lot of money on a small account.) Every HPA has the potential to be a very large profit contributor, and those that are not should be on your priority list to get them there.

HVA—High-Value Account: accounts with above average Gross Profit dollar production *and* a wide spread between

GM% and CTS% (meaning a high NBC%). HVAs are the smaller subset of HPAs that produce nearly all of the company's profits. HVAs are the accounts which get Concierge Customer Service, special pricing, dedicated resources, first call on inventory and services, and every benefit your company can provide to its most valuable accounts.

LIPA—Line-Item Profit Analytics: using highly granular (usually invoice line-item) profit to evaluate profits or losses in very small increments of transactional business

metric—number or statistic that can be compared to another similar statistic to evaluate the comparative value of each. There are several classes of metric:

- **activity metric**—first-order measure indicated by something that can be counted, such as; orders; picks (lines); invoices; shipments; headcount. Best used to assess resource requirement or consumption.
- **productivity metric**—first order dollar-related measures such as: revenue; gross profit; $CTS; $NBC; net profit. Best used to assess the scale of something like a branch, territory, or account.
- **rate metric**—second-order metric derived by combining two other metrics, usually by dividing one into another, such as: gross margin%; NBC%; $GP/invoice; CTS%; $GP/shipment; net profit %. Best used to assess relative efficiency.
- **time metric**—second- or third-order metric that indicates how a measure changes over time. Best used to assess progress that can indicates where the metric will go into the future. Time metrics are critical tools for executives responsible for future results.

NBC—Net Before Compensation: profit left after CoGS and CTS are deducted from revenue (revenue—CoGS—CTS)

NBC%—NBC Rate: percentage of revenue represented by the NBC (NBC ÷ revenue)

NBT—Net Before Taxes: the company's "bottom line"—earnings the company will pay taxes on (revenue—CoGS—CTS—sales comp)

Net—Net Profit: net or operating profit remaining after all operating expenses are covered
(revenue—CoGS—CTS—sales compensation)

Net%—Net Profit Rate: percentage of revenue represented by the Net (Net ÷ revenue)

P&L—Profit and Loss statement: standard financial statement, showing profit made or money lost during a specific time period. I recommend a specific layout that shows NBC.

	Rev (revenue)
–	**CoGS** (Cost of Goods Sold)
=	**GP** (gross profit)
–	**CTS** (Cost-To-Serve or operating expenses)
=	**NBC** (Net Before Sales Compensation)
–	Sales Comp
=	**NBT** (Net Before Taxes)

PDA—Profit-Drain Account: accounts with above average Gross Profit dollar production *and* an inverted spread between GM% and CTS% (CTS% is higher than GM% producing a negative NBC%). PDAs are the accounts which need to be reformed or dropped, as they consume previously-made profits with each transaction.

PIP—Peak Internal Profit: the total profit generated by only the money-making invoice lines

QPM—Quantum Profit Management: an advanced management philosophy and practice where very granular profit results are used to drive strategies and tactics that drive large numbers of incremental improvements in profitability

SKU—Stock Keeping Unit: a single, orderable item in your company's selection of products and services offered to customers

WayPoint—WayPoint Analytics is the cost and profit analytical system companies use to monitor and manage the programs, processes and strategies laid out in this book

Acknowledgements

This book, and the work it's based on, wouldn't be possible without the mentoring and assistance of many people.

First, I'd like to thank Bruce Merrifield for his generosity in sharing perhaps the best and broadest inventory of profit-driving strategies and tactics in existence. The man is a walking encyclopedia of best practices, and has spent over four decades collecting, analyzing and refining knowledge of what actually works.

This book would not exist without the brilliant insights and courageous actions of distribution company executives that use WayPoint Analytics, and where I can identify and quantify the profit changes their ideas have produced. I'm honored to know you and include you in my list of friends.

I'd also like to thank my editor, Joseph Glad, who invested many hours in the raw transcripts for this book. If I seem particularly articulate, it's purely due to his work in untangling my original thoughts, deleting my verbal ticks, and assembling the rough text into something most readers would appreciate.

Finally, Jean Perkins and Diane MacLean for the tedious work of proofing the text, picking out my many typos, mis-edits and verbal ticks. Thank you both for the many embarrassments that would surely have been pointed out by my readers.

About WayPoint

WayPoint Analytics is an online system used by wholesale distribution companies to closely measure and manage their profitability.

WayPoint will hold a rolling three years of your company's invoice data, freshen it on a weekly or monthly basis, and load your quarterly P&L statements. The system distributes all of your expenses throughout the invoices, costing your business out in fine detail.

WayPoint produces hundreds of detailed profit reports—covering every aspect of profit management for every aspect of your business. The reports are accessible via the Internet from your desktop, your home, or on the road on your smart phone or tablet.

WayPoint clients have posted 100%, 300% and 500% profit gains by having the insights given to them through the WayPoint reports into how and where their companies make and lose money. These insights have rendered them free to act to pass their competitors by.

I'd be delighted to discuss your business or answer your questions. If you and your team would like to see WayPoint Analytics for yourself, please call us
or visit our website at:
www.waypointanalytics.com

About the Author

Randy MacLean is the founder and President of WayPoint Analytics, a software-in-the-cloud company that serves the wholesale distribution industry. An expert in the field of distribution analytics and profitability, Randy is a frequent presenter to wholesale distribution associations across the US and Canada.

He is a co-founder of the Advanced Profit Innovation Conference (APIC), an annual two-day accredited educational conference where the top experts in distribution profitability meet to teach each other (and a select group of distribution executives) best practices and what's coming next.

Using WayPoint and working with hundreds of business owners and managers, Randy's been focused on providing the deep analytics needed to identify and control the millions of profit increments which exist and are lost in a typical business.

He's partnered with Bruce Merrifield, and together they've spent most of the last decade helping distribution executives recognize and capture the enormous, but largely unrealized, profits existing in every distribution company.

In his off time, Randy is a skilled shooter, an NRA Certified Instructor, and enjoys ballroom dancing with his wife, Diane.

A native of Canada, he's been a resident of Scottsdale, Arizona for over 20 years, where he enjoys year-round summer-style living with his wife and their dogs.

To find out more about Randy MacLean, visit him at www.randymaclean.com or www.waypointanalytics.com

Made in the USA
Middletown, DE
04 August 2016